WHAT OTHERS ARE SAYING...

"It has been a great joy of mine to know Randy Lawrence. Randy is a 'Noah' in a world overcome by darkness. He is a young man *in pursuit*. In this great book, Randy challenges the reader to pursue the right things—the needful things in life. I pray Randy's book will challenge you, as it has me, to pursue God's presence and power, through your own purity, purpose and prayer."

Dr. Larry Martin, River of Revival Ministries
Author of multiple books
www.drlarrymartin.com

"There's an awakening among leaders today to cultivate a deeper relationship with God. The Holy Spirit is raising up a new generation of people who are pursuing God with everything; Randy's book provides key insights for the 'Noah's of the last days.' This book is a great resource for not only pastors but for every Christian who has a desire to go beyond the superficial. I am convinced that this book has the potential to change your life and rejuvenate your passion for God.

Josh Pennington, Senior Pastor Christpoint Church
Galena, Kansas

"Randy and I had the privilege of working in ministry together for several years. One of his personal characteristics and strengths is competition. What I love, is that Randy writes like he lives, and that is in fierce competition against an enemy that does not want us to Pursue our purpose. If you like average don't pick this book up, but if you want a greater understanding of how to keep passionately progressing in your walk with God as a leader, then give this a read."

Joe Skiles, Lead Pastor New Hope Church
Concord, California

IN PURSUIT

RANDY K. LAWRENCE

PRINTS

Published by MPRINTS Publishing
PO Box 850
Joplin, Missouri 64801

Printed in the United States of America

First Printing, 2017

ISBN: 978-1-5323-4406-0

DEDICATION

To my Wife, who has been so supportive during every twist and turn this amazing God-journey has taken us on.

CONTENTS

Foreword   1

Introduction   5

PART 1
THE DEFINITION OF PURSUIT

CHAPTER 1: *As It Was in the Days of Noah*   13

CHAPTER 2: *The Defining Mark of Pursuit*   25

CHAPTER 3: *The Refining Mark of Pursuit*   37

CHAPTER 4: *The Aligning Mark of Pursuit*   49

CHAPTER 5: *The Assigning Mark of Pursuit*   63

CHAPTER 6: *The Shining Mark of Pursuit*   77

PART 2
THE DECLARATION OF PURSUIT

INTRODUCTION: *Intro to Part 2*   89

CHAPTER 7: *In Pursuit of Purpose*   95

CHAPTER 8: *In Pursuit of Presence*   109

CHAPTER 9: *In Pursuit of Prayer*   121

CHAPTER 10: *In Pursuit of Purity*   133

CHAPTER 11: *In Pursuit of Power*   145

CHAPTER 12: *Conclusion (Chop-Chop)*   157

Endnotes   161

Acknowledgments   165

About the Author   167

FORE-WORD

My covenant friend, Randy Lawrence Jr., has written a dangerous book. It is dangerous, first of all, because of its content. It is an honest, compelling assessment concerning the condition of today's Church. Randy's intentional synthesis concerning "as it was in the days of Noah, so it will be at the coming of the Son of Man" from Matthew 24:37 is a clarion call for every Christ-follower to live *In Pursuit* of the Christ-life.

Fortunately, those who accelerate their spiritual pace can't help but open themselves to the unfathomable nature of God. The term "unfathomable" alludes to the open sea or ocean. When seafarers determined to measure the depth of an ocean, they used a unit of measure called a fathom—a nautical unit of about six-feet in length created from the sound reflecting off the bottom of the ocean. When something is deemed as "unfathomable," the bottom of the ocean is so far down that the sound never returns when sent out. What a powerful word picture of our journey of faith. Our all-out pursuit of God only enhances the unfathomable nature of His divine providence at work in our lives.

Second, this book is dangerous because it exposes an unbiblical philosophy called "backwards Christian soldiers" pervading the Church today. This world's system may push the pendulum toward "gross darkness," but when the Church is *In Pursuit*, it is not on the defensive, but the offensive. In other words, the Church shouldn't be spending an inordinate amount of time trying to stop Hell, but Hell should be spending an inordinate amount of time trying to stop the Church. In fact, the assertion of "who's stopping whom" speaks to what side of the tracks we're really on. If Hell is stopping us, then we aren't building what Jesus is building because Jesus said, "I am building my Church, and Hell can't stop it" (Mt. 16:18).

In the very first prophecy of the Bible, God prophesied that Satan may bruise the woman's heel, but received a crushed head in the process. Here's some great news! When we are *In Pursuit*, we are not playing the role of the crushed head; we're playing the role of the bruised heel. In other words, we may experience some bruising along the way, but we are still the ones doing the crushing.

Third, this book is dangerous because it is not to be read, but experienced. Reading this book for mental stimulation won't work because it provides practical steps toward transformation. The quick-hitting antidotes and personal stories, such as the "Fig-Newton boy" and "this isn't preschool anymore," will "connect the dots" for real-time, real-life change.

Finally, this book is ultimately dangerous because of who has written it. Randy is a man who has proven himself. Anyone who spends time with him recognizes a divine connection and a personal commitment to live as a man *In Pursuit*. This book, which is really an alarm clock blaring with truth, comes from the heart of one who is hearing the intensity of the sound along with us. With vulnerability and focused intensity, he is calling for us to become much more than we are—a greater version of ourselves in Christ.

Candidly, *In Pursuit* is really a devotional guide. First, because it accurately describes what we all know but don't want to admit; many of us are complacent. Second, because it provides personal reflection and potent revelation, we can no longer live in ignorance, parked in our passive faith. And third, because the messenger is living the message in front of us, he compels us toward overcoming any dissonance that we have between contemplation and activation.

This practical book is a serious remedy for all status quo, maintenance-mode Christian living. It is for those with "ears to hear" and who are committed to an all-out pursuit in the "last days of the last days." Randy Lawrence Jr. and I have committed ourselves to live as people *In Pursuit*. Our pray is that many more will join us.

Dr. Wayman Ming Jr.
Founder and President of Exceed International

INTRO

My soul pursues you . . .

-King David

There came a time in the history of the Jewish people, when the Lord gave in to their pleas and decided to give them a king. So the prophet Samuel—the man of God—sets out to anoint Israel's first king.

The scriptures record in 1 Samuel 10 that the Lord chose a man of the house of Kish named Saul. However, there was one small problem; on coronation day, the people couldn't find him. So they inquired of the Lord as to just exactly where their new king was, to which the Lord replied: *"There he is hidden among the equipment"* (vs. 22).

Many of you picking up this book feel like this. You feel hidden in the "stuff" of this world. Deep down inside, you have a burning desire to do something great with your life and fulfill the purposes and plans that God has for your life—but you feel hidden.

Lost in the stuff.

Hidden in the clutter and confusion of this day and age. This world that we live is BRUTAL, and it seems to get worse with each passing day. It becomes very easy for us to lose sight of the purposes and plans of God.

God has an anointing for your life, and He desires to use your life to accomplish great things, but it's easy to get hidden among the equipment.

Some of you picking up this book even feel like you are lost in the "stuff" of ministry. At one point you were "all in" on your willingness for God to use your life in whatever way He saw fit—send me to Africa, Asia, New York—I'll go wherever you want me to go and do whatever you want me to do. But now you're confused from the clutter and chaos of your experiences. In the midst of the daily grind, you've lost sight of your divine destiny and have become hidden in the equipment.

I have news for you—a proclamation to speak over your life by the power of the Holy Spirit: "It's time to come out."

NOW is the time for you to arise and be *in pursuit*. Come out from the stuff. Your days of hiding are over; there is greatness on the inside of you!

So what is this book about? What does *in pursuit* even mean?

In the next few pages, I hope to explain what *in pursuit* means and all it encompasses. But first, let me share with you my prayer for this book. I pray that this would be a modern day manifesto of those radical followers of Christ who will be *in pursuit*, and as a result help usher in the greatest move of God that our world has ever seen—beyond anything we could ask or imagine.

Are you ready? Let's go for it. It's time to be *in pursuit!*

DEFI

P

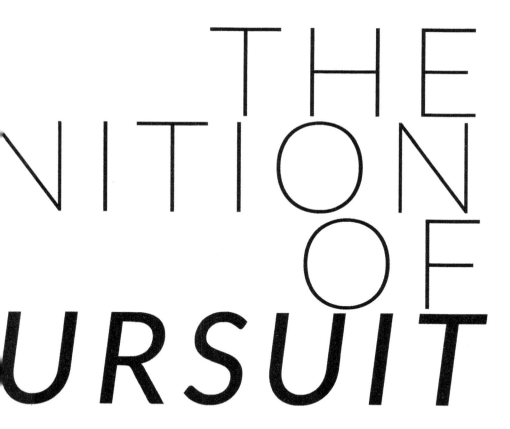

THE DEFINITION OF PURSUIT

CHAPTER 1

As It Was In The Days Of Noah

As it was in the days of Noah, so it will be at the coming of the Son of Man.

–Matthew 24:37 | NIV

1

"As it was in the days of Noah." Have you ever heard this phrase before?

Growing up, I was a PK (Pastor's Kid), which meant that I was in church services all the time. And when I mean all the time—I mean ALL the time.

We had church services on Sunday morning. Services—plural. That's right. Long before the modern-day concept of "multiple" Sunday morning services or "experiences," we had already beaten church strategists to the punch when you factored in Sunday School.

Back in the day, Sunday School was like a service! We had our own preacher, prayer requests, illustrations (killer felt-board style). Hey, we even took up our own offering. Truth be told our Sunday School was probably longer than the average Sunday morning worship services of today.

Then we still had Sunday night, Wednesday night, Tuesday night prayer meeting—PLUS the regularly scheduled Revival services. The bottom line is: I was in church a lot, and I heard a ton of preaching. As a result, from a young age I was very familiar with the words *"As it was in the days of Noah."*

Preachers would use this phrase or verse when preaching about "The Last Days." That's another aspect of growing up in church back then that's quite different from most churches today in that you don't hear of much preaching on the "Last Days" anymore. Back in the day, however, churches—especially Pentecostal churches—were always preaching about the Last Days. Preachers would talk about the rapture and the need to be ready because nobody, and I mean nobody, wanted to be left behind!

Plus, there were more than just sermons about the Last Days. There where dramas, songs, skits—and even full-fledged church productions—all on the Last Days and the rapture of the church! I still remember one of the songs from one of those church dramas I saw as a kid:

> *Life was filled with guns and war,*
> *And all of us got trampled on the floor;*
> *I wish we'd all been ready.*
> *Children died, the days grew cold,*
> *A piece of bread could buy a bag of gold;*
> *I wish we'd all been ready.*
> *There's no time to change your mind;*
> *The Son has come and you've been left behind.*[1]

Just reading the lyrics gives me chills! It makes me remember sitting as a kid in the church pew, scared half to death thinking, "There ain't no way I'm missing the rapture! Nope, not this dude. NO WAY, JOSÉ!" I remember not long after one of those dramas coming back inside my house after playing outside and not immediately seeing anyone . . .

"Hello?? Mom? Dad? Where is everyone at? Oh no! This is what that song was about!!"

The worst, however, was waking up in the middle of the night and thinking to myself, "It's way too quiet in this house—oh, snap, I'd better go check Mom and Dad's room to make sure I didn't miss the rapture!"

Growing up, my little Pentecostal church might not have done everything right, but one thing they did quite well was putting the fear of God in ya'!

And then who can forget the movies? The low-budget, cheesy rapture movies. Let me just say that the Christian movies of today have come a long way from the rapture movies of the '80s and '90s; something we can all be thankful for.

The bottom line is this: There was a ton (and I mean a ton) of attention on the "Last Days" and what it would look like, and one of the most common passages used was this one from Matthew's Gospel: *"As it was in the days of Noah . . ."* This was the description that Christ used as a key indicator of what the Last Days would look like.

THE FIRST HALF

So what was it like "in the days of Noah"? A quick glimpse of the scriptures, gives some indicators as to what Noah's days where like—therefore indicating what the "Last Days" would look like. Take note of the *vivid descriptors*:

> *The LORD observed the extent of **human wickedness** on the earth, and he saw that everything they thought or imagined was **consistently** and **totally evil**. So the LORD was sorry he had ever made them and put them on the earth. **It broke his heart**.* (Genesis 6:5-6, NLT)

> *Now God saw that the earth had become **corrupt** and was **filled with violence**. God observed all this corruption in the world, for everyone on earth was corrupt.* (Genesis 6:11-12, NLT)

Wickedness, violence, corruption, consistently evil. . . . Does this sound familiar to anyone? Sounds to me like the daily CNN Breaking News feed. I don't need to pull out statistics to prove to anyone that has had a pulse over the last 30 days to try to convince you that the day and hour in which we live is, *"as it was in the days of Noah."* The descriptors are pretty much identical.

There are some days when even just hearing of some wretched account of hatred or violence that has occurred on our planet, that my heart is just filled with pain.

"Who could do this?"

"How does this happen?"

Just hearing the stories hurts, almost to the point of making you go numb. I can't even begin to imagine how it makes the Lord feel. Perhaps it brings about some of the same emotions He experienced in Noah's day when he said, *"I am sorry I ever made them"* (Genesis 6:7).

But yet that is just one-half of the equation.

That's right, one-half.

To be honest with you though, that is the only half of the equation that I'd ever thought of when I considered this prophetic description of the last days. To me this was my theology of this description:

> *As it was in the days of Noah = The world was gonna go cray-cray and people were going to absolutely lose their minds caught up in their evil deeds. Darkness, darkness, darkness. Pain, shame, gloom & despair. End of story.*

This was the only side of the coin that I was looking at.

That was until the Lord began to speak to my heart about the topic of *pursuit.*

THE MISSING PIECE

As the Spirit of God began to speak to me about pursuit, he prompted me to read the story again, and this time play closer attention. When I did, it was like an explosion went off inside of my spirit as I saw what I had missed.

The violence, wickedness and evil of Noah's time, that's just one indicator of the Last Days. The second indicator though is what I was missing; I wasn't seeing it at all. Take note of its **vivid descriptors**:

> *But Noah found **favor with the LORD**. This is the account of Noah and his family. Noah was a **righteous man**, the only **blameless** person living on earth at the time, and he **walked in close fellowship with God**. (Genesis 6:8-9, NLT)*

Noah wasn't caught up in the cesspool culture of his day. He wasn't going with the flow. He wasn't lowering his standards. He wasn't caught up in the complacency of the hour. He wasn't losing his mind like everyone else. He was laser focused on the task at hand.

He wasn't concerned with being politically correct, or appealing to the cultural norms of his day. In a day and hour when everyone around him was breaking the father heart of God, Noah was walking in close fellowship with God.

While they were shameless, he was blameless.

While their acts were lowly, his were holy.

While they were living like the devil, he was on another level.

Are you seeing the picture? Let me put it another way. He was *IN PURSUIT.*

Hebrews gives us another vivid description of Noah:

> *By **faith** Noah, being divinely warned of things not yet seen, **moved with godly fear**, prepared an ark for the saving of his household.* (Hebrews 11:7)

We see that Noah was a great man of faith, but not only did he *have* faith, he *did something* with his faith! HE MOVED. He was *in pursuit*. I love how the writer of Hebrews describes Noah's pursuit, "*he moved with godly fear.*"

The KRV (King Randy Version) says, "He had some GODLY FEAR in his REAR, and he put a move on it!" You see Noah stood out in the day and hour in which he lived. He was on a mission. He was moving. He was building, dreaming, pushing, reaching—believing that God had a divine plan and purpose for his life. While society seemed to be crumbling around him, Noah was laser-focused on God's assignment for the day and hour in which he lived.

He was *IN PURSUIT*.

He had more than a pep in his step, he had some fear in his rear—a healthy fear that kept him *in pursuit*, walking in close fellowship with God.

ONE BIG BUT

This was the side of the story that I was missing! I was missing the best part. I was so focused on the bad descriptors of the "last days" that I was missing the best descriptors. All too often this is the case in our Christian circles—we give so much attention to all that is wrong or ungodly in our world that it almost becomes the apex of our mindset on the day and hour in which we live. We fixate on the bad, when we should be drawn to the best. Often the bulk of our sermons are spent on pointing out all that is wrong in our world. We are so focused on the wickedness, the vile acts, the sheer hatred that breaks the heart of God, that we miss out on what I believe the Spirit wants to direct our attention to, which we find in verse 8: "*But Noah.*"

That's right.

But Noah.

I love the "buts" in the Bible. There are some amazing buts in the Bible, and this one in particular is off the charts.

Immediately after the Lord expresses his feelings on the wickedness of the hour, even confessing the emotion that He regrets creating mankind, the story takes a sudden turn with two words—BUT NOAH.

Let me help you with a simple definition of what the word "BUT" means. I describe this conjunction as follows:

> What you've just read or heard is very important, however (BUT). what you're getting ready to read or hear next is the most important thing you need to know. It's a bright, flashing, LED light that communicates: "Don't miss this next part, it's the highlight."

Perhaps this will give you a deeper understanding of the word.

Johnny and Sally are best friends. One day Sally gets one of those fancy folded-up letters (made from a page ripped out of your science notebook) that middle school girls in the '90s dreamed of. After undoing all the fancy folds, she opens up the creased notebook paper to read the message she's been waiting for:

> "Will you go out with me?
>
> ☐ YES ☐ NO or ☐ Maybe."

She quickly pulls out her #2 pencil and with a big smile checks:

☑ YES ☐ NO or ☐ Maybe.

From that day on she and Johnny are a thing! They are the most talked about couple in junior high. Everyone is jealous of their relationship; everyone aspires to have a dreamy romance like Johnny & Sally. And then one day Sally tells Johnny she needs to "talk."

She takes a deep breath, stares into his eyes and starts, "Johnny, you are the sweetest guy I've ever met. You carry my tray at lunch; you walk me to every class and open every door. You text all the right messages and emojis and send me the sweetest snaps. Johnny, I don't know how else to say this: you are everything I've ever dreamed of having in a boyfriend, BUT . . . (*dramatic pause*)"

You see when Johnny hears the word, "BUT," he knows what is coming next. And what is coming next is the most important part of the conversation!

She continues, "But, I just want to be friends."

BOOM.

There it is. Johnny just got dropped like a bad habit. You see, he realized that regardless of all of the nice things Sally said about him, when she threw in "BUT," what was coming next was the EPICENTER of the story.

BUT NOAH.

I believe this is what the Spirit is saying in regard to the day and hour in which we live. Yes, there will be dark days filled with wickedness and numbing evil, BUT that is not the end of the story, AND that is not the highlight of the story either. I hear the Spirit saying, "Wake up and see the other side of the equation—BUT NOAH."

God is raising up sons and daughters filled with God's grace and favor who will be in radical pursuit of the things of the Lord! They will not be sidetracked or intimidated by the spirits of this age. They will not back down from what is seemingly impossible. They will have some GRIT about themselves. Like Noah, they will be filled with faith and move with godly fear to accomplish the task that God set them on this earth to do.

THEY WILL BE *IN PURSUIT*.

I don't know about you, dear friend, but I want in on this. SIGN ME UP.

I'm ready to say Yes. Yes, God, I want to be used by you in these last days, and I am ready to be *IN PURSUIT*.

That is what this book is all about. It is a commissioning of sorts, a rallying cry to the spiritual Noah's of our day (men and women) who are rising up out of the darkness of this hour with the shining light of God's favor and grace as they live a life *IN PURSUIT*.

As it was in the days of Noah.

Are you ready to be a fulfillment of this ancient prophecy? If so, I believe the Spirit of God is ready to take you on a journey, one beyond your wildest imagination. A radical journey of being *in pursuit*, where God anoints you with such incredible favor and grace, as he did with Noah—to accomplish what is seemingly impossible in the natural realm that many may be saved.

As it was in the days of Noah . . . on your mark, get set, let's go for it! *IN PURSUIT*.

THE DEFINING MARK OF PURSUIT

*These who have turned the
world upside down..."*

-Acts 17:6 | NKJV

2

PURSUIT.

One word, so simple, but yet so defining.

I am in pursuit.

You are in pursuit.

We all are in pursuit.

The question is, what are we *in pursuit* of? What is it that has captivated our hearts, minds, and souls? What is it that causes us to wake up every morning and gives us a reason for living? What is it that motivates us, pushes us, and even at times sustains us through the difficult seasons in life and refreshes us in the good times?

In a world where every moment of every day something is lobbying for our attention—a tweet, a text, a snap—what is it that has captured you? What is the *one thing*, that when someone says your name, immediately pops into their mind?

Let's play a little game. I'm going to list an establishment, and I want you to list the first thing that comes to your mind when you think of it.

Burger King _____.
Dallas Cowboys _____.
Nike _____.
Apple _____.
Starbucks _____.
Chick-Fil-a_____.

Here are my answers:

Burger King — Whopper.
Dallas Cowboys — Football (or an attempt).
Nike — Shoes.
Apple — Computers.
Starbucks — Coffee.
Chick-Fil-a — Heaven. (I'm positive it will be there, right? But closed on Sunday of course).

Although I'm sure you and I probably didn't have the exact same answers, we were probably close or similar. My point is that in our minds these establishments have left a distinct impression, and while they might make us think of many things, there is *ONE thing* that really stands out.

For example Starbucks, perhaps some of you immediately thought:

"Carmel Macchiato."
"Peppermint Mocha Frappuccino."
"Pumpkin Spice Latte."
(Should I stop now?)

Others may have thought of:

"Seattle."
"Cool Mugs."
or "Over-Priced."

While many things could come to your mind, there is one thing that is the overarching, defining mark of Starbucks, and that is coffee. It is what they are known for. It is, what I would propose as, their *pursuit*.

Paul wrote to the church at Philippi, and he said, *"Brethren, I do not count myself to have apprehended; but one thing I do, forgetting those things which are behind and reaching forward to those things which are ahead, I press toward the goal for the prize of the upward call of God in Christ Jesus"* (Philippians 3:13-14).

Paul is essentially saying, there is ONE THING that I am *in pursuit* of.

One thing I am captivated by.

One thing I am passionate about.

One thing that I will be defined by.

Yes, it is true Paul was actively involved in many different activities or functions in his life. We know from reading his activity in the book of Acts that he wasn't just a preacher/missionary, but he also at times worked a job as a tentmaker. My point, however, is that although there were many things that Paul was engaged in, there was *one thing* that stood out from everything else. One thing that He would be remembered for. One thing that he was striving, pressing, reaching for—*in pursuit* of, and that pursuit was his blank.

Paul — _____.

It was his coffee, his computer, his shoes.

So what is the *defining mark* of pursuit? The defining mark of pursuit speaks of our PASSION. It speaks to the one thing that permeates through every fabric of our being. What is that one thing that everyone around you knows beyond a shadow of a doubt you are first and foremost passionate about?

I believe with all of my heart that God is desiring to awaken something inside his followers—something that perhaps we've lost somewhere along the way—that being the *defining mark* of pursuit which is PASSION.

If we can rediscover or awaken the passion of our pursuit, it will radically transform the world in which we live.

Bummer Of A Birthmark

Ever heard the phrase, "That's gonna leave a mark!"?

As a father of four young, rambunctious children that is a line that is repeated often in our home. More often in fact than I care to admit. I'm not sure where my kids get all of their insanity from; however, I've got a one-inch childhood scar on my forehead that provides me with a daily clue as to where the hyper genes come from!

It was said of the early disciples, "These are the ones who have turned the world upside down" (Acts 17:6). They left a mark on the world in which they lived! As the gospel spread and the early disciples went from town to town, their reputations preceded them. They made a difference. They changed the world. Make NO MISTAKE about it, they had the defining mark of pursuit—PASSION. And as a result, their pursuit left a mark. It turned the world upside down!

Long before the early disciples we read about in the New Testament, Noah was doing the same thing: his pursuit left a mark on history. As we just discussed, Paul understood the power of pursuit. He understood that our pursuit becomes a legacy—what we are remembered for, our mark left here on earth.

Even in the closing verses of his letter to the Church at Galatia, Paul states, "I bear in my body the *marks* of the Lord Jesus" (Galatians 5:17).

While Paul is making a point of refuting claims that the disciples in Galatia should have to be physically "marked" by the law of circumcision, he is also at the same time stating the very plain fact that his physical body did actually bear the marks of his commitment to Jesus Christ.

Paul's passion—his pursuit of Jesus had caused him to bear in his physical body marks of his commitment (beating, persecution, etc.). He had proof of his dedication to the Lord Jesus. What point am I trying to make?

What I'm saying is that just like the apostle Paul, *our pursuit should leave a defining mark in the world in which we live.* Everyone around us should know what we are about. And while we may not physically bear marks, we metaphorically bear the defining mark of pursuit—PASSION.

One of my favorite cartoons of all time was created by Gary Larson, featured in his cartoon "The Far Side." This particular cartoon featured two deer facing each other in the forest. One of the deer has a very distinctive birthmark on his chest—a bull's eye in fact. The second deer is staring at him with a concerned look on his face, in which the caption reads, "Bummer of a birthmark, Hal!"

Cheesy I know, but I love it!

You see, your pursuit becomes a defining mark on your life. It becomes like Hal's birthmark, causing you to stand out from the crowd. It becomes like one of those bright flashing LED store lights that reads, "This is what this person is all about."

The reason we are marked by our pursuit, is because our pursuit marks us. Let me say that again so it can sink in a little more:

The reason we are marked by our pursuit, is because our pursuit marks us.

Paul explained this concept clearly, in Philippians 3:12, "*Not that I have already attained, or am already perfected; but I press on, that I may lay hold of that for which Christ Jesus **has also laid hold of me.***" (Philippians 3:12, NKJV) Paul is essentially saying, "I'm *in pursuit* of that which has already laid hold of me! It has marked me!" The reason Paul went on to talk about his ONE THING, was because that ONE THING had already marked HIM! Paul was marked by his pursuit, because his pursuit had marked him.

I believe with all of my heart that in this day and hour in which we live God is awakening inside of his people the defining mark of *pursuit*: PASSION.

It defines us.

It becomes what we are known for.

And the passion of our pursuit becomes a clear indicator to our world, that we are in the Last Days.

A Trip To The Nurses' Station

I'll never forget the Summer of 2004. I was leading worship at a camp in one of my favorite places in the world, Spencer Lake Christian Camp in Waupaca, Wisconsin. It was the very first morning of camp, and we were having a staff orientation before all of the campers arrived. The room was filled with about 150 staff members, and as always at this particular camp the atmosphere was just buzzing with excitement and anticipation for the week.

After opening with a song of worship, I returned to my seat for the rest of orientation. They asked the nursing staff for the week to come up front for their portion of orientation, and that is the moment when my life completely changed forever.

It was in this moment—this one shining moment—that—BOOM!—I laid eyes on the most beautiful women I had ever seen in my life.

She was introduced as one of the nurses for the week, and I immediately fell ill. That week I set a record for the number of visits to the nurses' station! I came down with everything—headache, fever, splinter, rash—I even looked for sick people to volunteer to escort them to the nurses' station.

I was in love.

This young, beautiful, soft-spoken lady—full of God's grace—had captivated my heart and I was *IN PURSUIT*.

Make no mistake about it, I totally had the defining mark of pursuit—PASSION. I was passionately in love with this girl. So much in fact, that in just a little over three months after that camp ended, I would ask Dawn to marry me, and as they say, the rest is history!

You see, the things we are passionate about and *in pursuit* of, set a direction for us in life—this is where I'm headed, this is what I'm about. It begins to define us. They cause us to prioritize differently, to get out of our comfort zone moving towards the goal set before us. Our pursuit sets a defining course for our life.

My One Thing

Stop for a moment right now and think about your life. Regardless of whether you are 13 or 113, I want you to think about your life. What is it that comes to your mind? What is that one thing, that defining mark? Go ahead, fill in the blank:

_____: _____.

(*your name*)

What is the blank for you?

What is your pursuit?

By the way, there's no middle ground here. There's no "I'll grab a cheap ticket and sit up in the stands and watch this one play out." *You are always pursuing something.* Remember, the question is NOT *am* I in pursuit? But rather *what am I* in pursuit of?

For many of us perhaps there are many words or things that come to mind, perhaps it just depends on what time frame of your life you reflect on. Some of us make different choices than others, some of us have different upbringings that have drastic effects on our lives. Regardless, our journeys are all different.

The point, however, is that in our lives we are always pursuing something and that something, that _____, becomes a defining part of our life. And while there may be many things that we engage in, there is that one thing that pushes itself to the front and takes precedence over everything else.

It is what you are known for, remembered for, and ultimately defined as.

So what is your _____?

What is it that when people think of you they think of this one thing? This one passion, love, this radical pursuit.

As you meditate on this question, let me end this chapter by redirecting you to another question—one that is actually of greater importance—and that is, *"what should my pursuit be?"*

One day when surrounded by a crowd of people, a lawyer asked Jesus a very important question, "What is the greatest commandment?" In other words, what must be our priority, our foundation, our pursuit? His response was simple,

> *"You shall love the Lord your God with all your heart, with all your soul, and with all your mind." This is the first and great commandment. And the second is like it: "You shall love your neighbor as yourself." On these two commandments hang all the Law and the Prophets. (Matthew 22:37-40)*

I propose to you that in this passage Jesus lays out a model for what our pursuit should look like; He helps define it:

A relentless love for God and the things He loves.

So simple. But yet so profound. I add the word relentless there because you get that feeling when you see Jesus use such strong words as "with *all your* heart, with *all your* soul, and with *all your* mind." You catch that defining mark of PASSION.

Jesus is pulling no punches here. He's not tippy-toeing around, or trying to be politically correct. He is painting a crystal clear picture of what our love for Him should look like: it requires EVERYTHING. It becomes our ultimate PASSION in life.

What should my ultimate pursuit be? What is it that I should be remembered for? What is it that, when someone says my name, they should immediately think of?

Answer: A relentless love for God and the things He loves.

This is our _____.
This is our goal.
This is our pursuit.
This is the mark we are shooting for and what we should be committed to, sold out for, and in radical pursuit of.

When everything is said and done and our time here on earth is finished, may it be said of us that this is what our pursuit was, a relentless love for God and the things He loves. May this passion be our defining mark. As we continue on in our journey through this book together, let us set our internal GPS to these coordinates and head in that direction.

Are you ready to be *in pursuit*?

Are you ready to possess the defining mark of pursuit?

CHAPTER 3

THE REFINING MARK OF PURSUIT

When Jesus is all you have,
Jesus will be all you need.

-Corrie Ten Boom

In the movie, *Serendipity*, there is a very inspiring and memorable quote that goes like this: "You know the Greeks didn't write obituaries. They only asked one question after a man died: 'Did he have passion?'"[1]

Now while there is no real substantial evidence to back up this supposed piece of Greek history, I still absolutely love this quote on passion. I like being around passionate people. Life's too short to be around duds all the time. Show me some passion!

The *defining* mark of pursuit that we just talked about in the last chapter speaks of just this, our passion. This is the side of pursuit that focuses on what we are passionate about, and that is what begins to define us. People know us for this; it becomes our story, our mark. However, that is just one side of pursuit.

Not only is there a *defining* mark of pursuit, but there is also a *refining* mark of pursuit. And while the *defining* mark of pursuit speaks to our passion, the *refining* mark speaks to something completely different, our *priorities*.

FIG NEWTON BOY

There was about one solid year in my life when I was 14-15 years old when I was *in pursuit* of one thing in life. I knew it, my family, friends, and everyone around me knew it. This thing motivated me, pushed me, and gave me passion to work harder than others.

I had always loved sports growing up. It was hard to find me without a ball of some type in my hand. Like many young kids I dreamed of the day of being a professional athlete with my poster hanging on every kid's wall and my sports figurine on their bedside table. However, as I got older, my dreams began to quickly vanish one sport at a time.

First basketball was out. "Too slow and can't jump," the coaches said, which is a nice way of saying, "How many fat white boys do you see in the NBA?" Next baseball diminished as I just lost a love for the game. I was just about to give up on it all when my last option began to show a glimmer of hope.

Some great friends from our church invited me to the gym to begin to work out. One of them was a sports trainer by trade, and he had just finished up leading another young man in our church through a pretty radical physical transformation. They knew that I had played football before but had simply lost interest. After joining them at the gym and actually really enjoying the workouts, I took on a new pursuit. With their experience and professional skills—combined with my size/frame, and decent athletic ability—they thought I had a shot over the next two years to develop into a collegiate athlete.

I was hooked.

This was my shot. So I set out on a journey, a pursuit. For the next ten months I was a gym rat. Every day I was in the gym after school, pushing myself hard. Weights, calisthenics, developing correct eating habits. The Twinkies and doughnuts were in the trash! I was determined to pursue nothing else. While others where spending their Saturday mornings playing video games, I was in the gym. My physical transformation was remarkable, losing 70 pounds in under ten months.

My commitment level was off the charts. In fact I specifically remember one day when we were out of school for some reason and I was at the church helping my parents with something. After a while my siblings and I got hungry, so we did what all PKs do (confession...), we raided the church food pantry. There, to our delight, we found some low-fat strawberry Fig Newtons which, coming from the food pantry, had probably expired ten months prior #yolo. Regardless of the expiration date we had found our snack, and I was so hungry that I ripped open the package and scarfed one down!

I immediately felt terrible.

I felt like such a loser.

"This isn't on my eating plan," I said to myself, "You know better; your trainer is going to be so disappointed." The internal conversation continued, "Play college football? Yeah, right Fig-Newton boy! FAT CHANCE."

Now, mind you, I had only eaten ONE Fig Newton, which is approximately a whopping 50 calories! But that was too much. Finally, I couldn't take the disappointment anymore, so I immediately got up from the table and went outside and ran a mile to make up for my momentary lapse in discipline!

You see this goal, this dream—was my pursuit in this season of life. It was priority numero uno. And it did more than just *define* me, it *refined* me. It was not only a *passion* but also a *priority*.

Now of course none of these things were bad. No, in fact many of them were great for me. Ditching the Twinkies and Krispy Kremes was GOOD. Trading the Ding Dongs for dumbbells was beneficial. Exercising and learning physical discipline were and are very healthy choices. These weren't BAD THINGS. They weren't going to send me to Hell. The problem was, they were my *priority*. They came first, and everything else took a back seat.

How many times do our pursuits—although they may be good, healthy and productive things—take priority in our lives over everything—including our relationship and pursuit of God?

I don't want you to misunderstand me. It's perfectly fine to be *in pursuit* of different things in life. We can be *in pursuit* of careers. We can be *in pursuit* of hobbies. We can be *in pursuit* of our favorite sports teams. All of this is fine—especially the sports teams (don't go messing with my sports)—however, what we have to ensure is that *nothing* takes precedence over our ultimate pursuit of God and the things He loves.

You see the *refining* mark of pursuit speaks to our *priorities*. It speaks to what comes *first* in our lives.

First Place

I am by nature a very competitive person. Growing up as a kid I loved to compete and was always very driven no matter what the competition was—to win. I wanted to come in first place. So it should have come as no surprise in my adult years when I took the Clifton Strengths Finder test, that out of the 34 classifications of strengths, my number one was COMPETITION.

At times this can be good and at times this can be very bad. There are many times while playing games in our home, when my wife has to give me that look, the look that says, "Hey, you do realize this is just Go Fish and 90% of your competition is under the age of nine?" My typical response is, "Sorry, suckers, somebody's gotta lose and today is your lucky day!"

You see, as a competitive person there is only one goal in mind: come in FIRST. It is the priority. Here is the thing about the refining mark of pursuit, it causes you to put God and the things of God FIRST.

Before every other love, passion, interest—even "good ones"—there is ONE thing that takes priority over everything else.

Make no mistake about it, this is in the DNA of what God had in mind when he created us to walk in fellowship with Him. In Exodus when God gave Moses and the children of Israel the ten commandments, what was the number one commandment?

You shall have no other gods before Me. (Exodus 20:3)

Plain and simple right? God is communicating the truth that He must come FIRST! But oh how easy it is to allow our priorities to get out of whack! Perhaps when you think of this commandment and the one that follows,

You shall not make for yourself a carved image—any likeness of anything that is in heaven above, or that is in the earth beneath, or that is in the water under the earth; you shall not bow down to them nor serve them. (Exodus 20:4-5a)

You think, "I'm good to go in this area. I'm not worshiping any golden statues or anything. I'm straight in this area. I worship at a church and not in my back yard to some golden calf or something." But, oh, how easy it is to have little g's in our life. It's the little g's that are so sneaky.

What is a little g?

No, I'm not talking about some thug gangsta, I'm talking about a god—(little) g.o.d. You see there is only one true big G. He's God and the only God. But there are lots of little g's—gods that if we're not careful can easily and quickly come before big G.

I've seen lots of idol worship in my day. I've seen little g's of sports teams, professions, hobbies, bass boats, people, jobs, ministries, etc. all take the place of big G in people's lives. Our hearts are often idol factories, pumping them out on a daily basis, continually competing for our time, love, and affections.

I think if we we're all honest, we would confess that at some point in life we've allowed other things to take the place of what should be the number one priority in life—our relentless pursuit of God and a relentless pursuit of the things He loves. Rather than Jesus sitting on the throne of our heart, we have turned that throne into a bench, and there He sits right alongside many other pursuits.

I've got some news for you: there's a side of God's character that is very similar to my Clifton Strength Finder Test, and that is this: He's concerned about FIRST PLACE.

Make no mistake about it, He wants to be first.

UNO.

Priority number one.

No, not in a mean sense of rub it in your face competitiveness, but a clear cut, "I want to be first." He goes on to say, *"For I, the LORD your God, am a jealous God"* (vs 5). How awesome is it that God is jealous of our pursuits? He wants to be first!

Why?

Because He has the absolute best in store for us! The plans He has for us the Bible says are "plans to prosper us and not to harm us, plans to give us a hope and a future" (Jeremiah 29:11, NIV).

Yes, He wants us to have the defining mark of pursuit which is passion, but he also desires for us to have the refining mark of pursuit which is priority.

THE REST OF THE STORY

So what happened to Fig Newton boy and his quest to become the next Division 1 College Football star? Well, right in the middle of my radical physical transformation, I experienced a spiritual transformation that forever changed my life.

It was much like Jacob's encounter with God in Genesis 32, where scripture records after the encounter that Jacob walked the rest of his life with a limp. He was forever changed. Everywhere he went, people could visibly see the difference in Jacob's life.

HE WAS TRANSFORMED.

This is exactly what happened to me. And in the middle of my encounter with God, I (just like Jacob) wrestled with God. Now, Jacob actually physically wrestled with the Lord; my match looked a little different.

As God began to reveal himself to me, He began to speak to me about the plans and the purposes He had for my future. I was overwhelmed. I thought, "Okay this is cool; I can do this when I'm older. I'm down with that. Right now I'm just 15 so I've got my whole life in front of me. I've got high school, college, etc., etc." But then the Lord began to press in on me a little to see how serious I was, to see if I really wanted it.

He showed me that He wanted me to start pursuing it right now. He wanted to be Priority Number One in my life. He wanted His plans to take priority and precedence over all of my plans. And He didn't want me to wait. I discovered that God doesn't delight in being put on hold.

My mind immediately began to think of the last ten months and all of the hard work and dedication I had put in to *my plans*. I still had a long way to go, but I had honestly never worked as hard towards something in my life as I had worked for that goal, for that pursuit. I knew what the Lord was asking me; He was asking me a simple question: "What pursuit will be your priority?"

I wrestled and wrestled with that. "I think I can do both, God! I can pursue my dream and Your dream. After all, I've got my entire life in front of me! Just let me have my high school years. After all, what about my friends and my trainer who have helped me and were counting on me? What would they think about all of this?"

He wanted a complete surrender.

He wanted to come first.

He wanted me to have faith that His plans were greater.

He wanted me to imagine what my life would look life if I gave the same effort, attention, and priority to Him and His plans, as I had to my own over the past ten months.

Maybe you're reading this and saying, "Wait a minute. Doesn't the Bible say that God will give us the desires of our heart? Why didn't you just go do what you wanted to do?"

Correct, the Bible does say that. Psalms 37:4 says,

Delight yourself also in the LORD,
And He shall give you the desires of your heart.

The key, however, to the desires of our heart coming to pass, is found in the first part of the verse, *"Delight yourself also in the LORD."* The Hebrew word for "delight" is, *"ânag,"* which means, *"to be soft or pliable."*

So catch this, when we are soft or pliable before the Lord, surrendering our will and heart to Him, our plans to His plans, we then line ourselves up for the desires of our hearts to come to pass! Anything else is just being stubborn and moving God from the throne of our heart to the bench of our heart.

So I had to come to a breaking point.

Here for me was the most incredible part of my God encounter. Even as the Lord revealed himself to me in such a powerful and personal way, that wasn't what blew me away. To me what amazed me the most was that even after all of the wrestling, I distinctly felt the Lord speak to me in the most loving and caring way: The choice is yours Randy.

You see God will never pressure us into something. He will never force something on us that we don't want. In His loving sovereignty the Lord still gives us a free will to choose.

So today, the choice is yours.

Will you surrender your plans to the Lord and allow him to become priority number one in your life? Will you sidestep the complacency and compromise of the day and hour in which we live and say Yes to the Lord?

Today is the day to say yes to the *refining* mark of pursuit which is *priority*.

THE ALIGNING MARK OF PURSUIT

Many things will catch your eye, but only a few things will catch your heart—pursue them.

–Jeanne Mayo

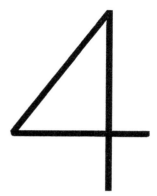

Few people in recent history have made such an impact on our culture as have Tim Tebow. Tebow has not only made a mark on the world with his distinguished athletic achievements, but he has also made an even larger impact with his outspoken faith. His passion for Christ is undeniable and it radiates through everything he does.

Tebow has used every platform that he's been given to share his faith in Jesus Christ, from his Heisman trophy winning days at the University of Florida, to defying all odds and playing in the NFL, to his career as a sports analyst with ESPN.

When Tebow announced in 2016 that he was going to pursue a career in professional baseball, a sport he had not played since high school, he had plenty of critics lining up to tell him how crazy he was. But once again, Tebow continued to defy the odds and signed his first contract with the New York Mets soon afterwards to play in the minor leagues.

Although the jury is still out as to whether Tebow will ever make it on a *major* league roster, he continues to prove even by making a minor league team, that his athleticism, work ethic, and dedication are off the charts.

With his latest career move to baseball, Tebow continues to use his platform to shine the light of Christ. In a press conference at First Data Field on Monday, February 27, 2017, Tebow was fielding questions about his upcoming goals and workout schedule with the Mets. One of the reporters began to question him as to whether or not all of his "off the field" pursuits where a distraction or hindrance to his potential baseball career. The reporter listed many of the charity efforts that Tebow has become known for through his foundation—asking how he could balance "those" passions while also trying to make a name for himself in baseball. His response, was once again a classic Tebow moment:

"At the end of the day, I know that's not why I'm here, it's not my biggest purpose, it's not my biggest calling, it's not how I want to be known in my life," Tebow said. "It's not as a football player, as a baseball player—as someone that worked hard to accomplish those things. I want my life to be so much more than that. I want to be someone that was known for bringing faith, hope, and love to those needing a brighter day in their darkest hour of need. That is something that is a life calling for me, and it is so much bigger than sports. But I am so grateful for sports because it's given me a platform to be able to share and love and care for people all over the world, so I wouldn't trade that for anything."[1]

I don't think the reporter was quite ready for Tebow's answer! It was in all honestly a very good question. How can someone be involved in so many things and be so passionate about all of them? Wouldn't something suffer? How does that work? How can you be passionate about so many things?

Really what the reporter was asking was, "With everything that you are involved in, Mr. Tebow, what is your ultimate pursuit? What is it that rises above everything else you are pursuing?"

This is a question that each and every one of us must come to grips with and be able to answer. In fact, as leaders it should be a question that we continually ponder. Tebow was able to answer it; he was crystal clear in the fact that, yes, while he may be involved in and passionate about many things, there was one ultimate purpose and calling and THAT was his ultimate pursuit.

Likewise we must be able to determine what our ultimate pursuit is.

I want to be crystal clear about something. It is perfectly okay to be passionate about many things in life. It's fine to have many things that we are "pursuing": careers, hobbies, relationships, dreams, even various aspects of "ministry." It is perfectly normal and fine to be passionate and *in pursuit* of all of these things (assuming of course that they line up with the word of God). The point, however, is that we must be able to test ourselves, or sit down behind the press room table and answer the question, "What is your *ultimate* pursuit?"

Here's something that will help you determine what your ultimate pursuit is, that which is taking first place over everything else. Let's play another "fill in the blank" game, but this time with multiple blanks. For fun, we'll call it the blankity-blank game. That's almost like Christian cussing right there!

So here we go; fill in the blanks:

My Passions in life:

1._____.
2._____.
3._____.

My Priorities in life:

1._____.
2._____.
3._____.

What is your ultimate pursuit?

The *answer*: It is what you put in line number one of both your *passions* AND your *priorities*. *You see it takes BOTH.*

In order for us to align ourselves with the definition of Pursuit that we defined earlier in this book as, "*A relentless love for God and the things He loves*," it takes an *alignment* of not only our passion, but also our priorities. God desires them both.

The *defining* mark of pursuit is—passion.

The *refining* mark of pursuit is—priorities.

The *aligning* mark of pursuit is when we learn to align both our passion and our priorities. It takes BOTH.

Let's look at it like this, I call this the equation of pursuit:

Passion + Priorities = Pursuit

When God is your top passion and God is your top priority, then He will be your ultimate "pursuit." When the defining mark of passion lines up with the refining mark of priorities, you, my friend, are *in pursuit*. As we read earlier, Hebrews 11 said of Noah, "*By faith Noah, being divinely warned of things not yet seen, moved with godly fear, prepared an ark for the saving of his household*," Hebrews 11:7. You see, Noah had the aligning mark of pursuit—both passion and priorities. Look at it:

"*By **faith** Noah...*" = PASSION

Was Noah passionate about his relationship with God? Absolutely. He was in fact so passionate about his faith that he makes it into the great "Hall of Faith" that this verse is pulled from in Hebrews chapter eleven. But that's not all. He also prioritized this faith—it moved him.

"*...moved with godly fear...*" = PRIORITIES

His love for God and the things of God also took precedence in his life. It moved him. You see it takes BOTH. Passion and priorities.

If, however, you remove one or the other out of the equation, you will end up with drastically different results:

Passion - Priorities = Burnout

You can be as passionate about God as you want, but unless you learn to prioritize God and the things of God in your life, you will find your pursuit quickly fading away. I love the defining mark of passion, but if you don't have the refining mark of priority, your fire will disappear faster than a doughnut at a Weight Watchers meeting!

How many times do we experience this in our lives? I would venture to say if you've been serving God for any length of time, then you (just like myself) have experienced this equation. Perhaps we attend a special event, a conference, or a revival, and God does something amazing in our lives. Our spirit is revived. We sense a renewing and our hearts are filled with passion! We're excited about worship, reading God's word, and prayer! We can't wait for the Church doors to open again for a corporate worship experience! We are on fire!!

We have the defining mark of pursuit—passion. The problem, however, is that when we don't learn to experience the *refining mark of priorities*, our passion eventually disappears! Without prioritizing your passion for God and the things of God, what happens is that this passion just eventually begins to fall in line with all of the other "passions" in our life. The result? That fiery, red hot passion we were experiencing quickly burns out.

Nobody wants a part of this—nor the reverse:

Priorities - Passion = Religion

This equation is terrible as well. This is dead and stale. With God as your priority, but yet with no passion, you will just be going through the religious motions. We don't need religious mannequins where everything looks real but there is absolutely no life. In this equation individuals still maintain a form of the things of God (His word, church attendance, prayer, etc), but they have lost their passion.

True, genuine pursuit, is when our priorities line up with our passions and vice versa. This is what will leave a mark in the day and hour in which we live. This is what will drive us, motivate us, and cause us to make a difference in the world.

It takes both.

It's not an either/or type of deal; it's a both/and.

Passion AND priorities.

Costco Saved My Life

Not too long ago my family and I stopped by our neighborhood Costco store for our weekly pilgrimage to the food section for free samples. Hey, with a family of six this is the cheapest meal of the week—FREE! I mean by the time you've made it over to the dessert section, you've seriously got a pretty decent meal. Thank you. Costco.

On this particular day they happened to be running a special on tires. Now I knew in my mind it wasn't quite time for new tires yet, but I decided on the way out to stop by and have the technicians take a look.

Upon inspecting my rear tires, the technician reported that I probably had a few thousand more miles, but he warned that it appeared my rear tires were wearing unevenly. I was about to thank him and head on out, but he insisted on checking the front tires (which I personally thought was a waste of time). He checked the first line of tread, "About the same," he reported, but then as he began to make his way further in, all of sudden he got a confused look on his face. Then his confusion turned into shock, as he looked up and said, "Man you've got wires bursting through the tread on the inside of your front tires—this is REALLY BAD!"

Why such a drastic difference?

Because I was out of alignment and I mean BAD out of alignment!

Too often the same happens with our passion and our priorities, we don't keep them in alignment. One or the other begin to drift down in rank.

Remember these lines?

My Passions in life:

    1._____.
    2._____.
    3._____.

My Priorities in life:

    1._____.
    2._____.
    3._____.

Here is what someone *in pursuit* looks like:

My Passions in life:

    1.<u>*God and the things of God.*</u>

    2._____.

    3._____.

My Priorities in life:

    1. <u>*God and the things of God.*</u>

    2._____.

    3._____.

"God and the things of God"—remember this comes from our target we set in the beginning of this book: *A relentless love for God and the things He loves.* To stay in alignment we must ensure that God and the things of God (in that *exact* order—relationship with God *before* the things of God), stay on line number one of BOTH our passions and our priorities. If we want to be a person that is truly *in pursuit,* we cannot afford for either one to drift down the ranking, taking a back seat to something else.

Noah, as we just read, had his passion and his priorities lined up. He not only had faith, but he also moved or acted on that faith. He walked not only in close fellowship with God, but he also walked in swift obedience to God—PASSION AND PRIORITIES.

This is what I believe the Spirit of God wants to awaken inside of the hearts and lives of the modern day Noahs. While the world may be ever increasingly known for its wickedness, volatility, and hatred, we will be known for our alignment of passion and priorities for God—our *pursuit.*

This alignment will not only leave a mark on the day and hour in which we live, but it will make history, it will change the world.

When you encounter an individual who has their passion and their priorities aligned, LOOK OUT! They are an immediate threat to the enemy. They don't just talk the talk, but they walk the walk.

I don't know about you, but I want God to align my passions and my priorities. I don't want to be out of alignment. I not only want the *defining* mark of pursuit on my life, but I also want the *refining* mark of pursuit! I want BOTH.

As I end this chapter, I want to end it with a powerful prayer prayed by Sir Francis Drake who was an English sea captain who lived from 1540–1596. I want you to allow the words to get deep in your spirit as you think about the alignment of your passion and your priority. We are asking God to shake us up—to disturb us! To awaken us to a radical pursuit like never before!

> Disturb us, Lord, when
> We are too pleased with ourselves,
> When our dreams have come true
> Because we dreamed too little,
> When we arrived safely
> Because we sailed too close to the shore.
>
> Disturb us, Lord, when
> With the abundance of things we possess
> We have lost our thirst
> For the waters of life;
> Having fallen in love with life,
> We have ceased to dream of eternity
> And in our efforts to build a new earth,

We have allowed our vision
Of the new Heaven to dim.

Disturb us, Lord, to dare more boldly,
To venture on wilder seas
Where storms will show Your mastery;
Where losing sight of land,
We shall find the stars.

We ask you to push back
The horizons of our hopes;
And to push back the future
In strength, courage, hope, and love.

This we ask in the name of our Captain,
Who is Jesus Christ.[2]

CHAPTER 5

THE ASSIGNING MARK OF PURSUIT

You weren't put on earth to be remembered. You were put here to prepare for eternity.

–Rick Warren

5

As I referred to earlier when I talked about my days in Sunday School, *most* churches today are drastically different from when I grew up. Now this is a very broad statement and I realize it doesn't apply to every church, but I would say for the majority of churches most of the changes have been positive and have positioned them to better reach today's world. I'm of course not referring to a change in *message*, but rather changes to *style* and *methods*.

One such classic example would be in the area of music. Most churches today—again I realize not all—but most have drastically changed how they do music from 20-30 years ago. Not just the style or genre of worship music, but also the presentation or performance of that music. I'm not talking about just transitioning from hymnals to worship choruses, but the church also has taken leaps and bounds in how we do music or worship.

Let me give you a classic example.

In most churches today you "try out" or "audition" for the worship team. This helps ensure that the individual desiring to help is actually somewhat gifted in the area in which they are desiring to lead others. So if you want to play an instrument or sing, there's a way to go about it; there's some structure now. Back in the day, especially in Pentecostal Churches—not so much!

You wanna sing? It's open mic night every time the doors are open!

Play the drums? Come on up, it's BYOS (bring your own sticks).

The crazy thing was, back in the day you didn't even have to come up on stage to be a part of the band! So let's say perhaps you always dreamed of being "in the band" but were terrified of going up on stage, there were instruments strategically placed all over the congregation that you could just grab at any time.

BOOM! You're in the band! I'm referring to—and I shudder as I type the word—a TAMBOURINE.

You might not have an OUNCE of musical talent or gifting in your body, but yet the tambourines were full access. You could see it in some people's eyes—just waiting for Sister Suzy to put that tambourine down so they could pounce on that sucker and fulfill their lifelong dream of being in the band. Many claimed the Spirit moved on them to pick up the tambourine. That I don't doubt! I just question what "spirit" they were moved by!

As you can imagine, the results were often . . . treacherous. Now I will say some people could legitimately play a tambourine, no ifs, ands, or buts about it. But for the most part, there were always one or two people (more on Sunday nights) who would grab that thing and not have a lick of timing.

In predominately white (Caucasian) churches this just magnified the timing and rhythm problems that we were already "blessed" with! You want to talk about a rhythm nightmare? Small Pentecostal Church, majority white, throw in some tambourines, and you've got some serious problems on your hands!

Such was the case for me on one Wednesday night. My father had asked me to lead the worship service on that night, which I was excited about but also a little nervous as well. Part of the nerves were because I was not only just starting to lead worship, but also still learning how to play the piano. And on this particular night, for the first time I was going to be actually leading and playing the piano at the same time.

I went in with a solid plan: "I'll just lean heavily on the band to carry things," I thought to myself, but wouldn't you know it, *not one member of the band showed up that night.*

So here I am, already nervous about leading worship, and also just an absolute beginner on the piano—faced with the task of being completely solo.

"How could this get any worse?" I thought. As a side note, if I could give you one piece of advice worth the price of this book it would be— NEVER say those words!

I was halfway into the first song and I was doing my best to "plunk" my way through it, when I had a "gracious" volunteer decide he wanted to get up and play the drums for me.

How nice. NOT!!!!!

My preschool plunking on the ivories, mixed with his absolute best attempt at something that resembled a beat, turned into an absolute disaster. I couldn't believe the nightmare I was in and it was only the first song. But, oh, just when I thought it was bad . . . BOOM, somebody picked up the tambourine!

You want to talk about off-the-charts chaos—it was on! I mean, if somebody would've had a video camera rolling that night, I'm sure we could have won some serious money off of America's Funniest Home Videos! Perhaps enough to purchase me some keyboard lessons!

Now I've shared these wonderful timbrel stories with you to point out that one of the greatest advancements we've experienced in a lot of church worship services is the creation of the *in-ear monitor systems.*

With such devices, musicians which used to have to try to hear themselves through a floor monitor while competing with other sounds from the congregations (i.e. tambourines), can now put in their isolation headphones and silence out the distractions.

Problem solved!

Not only does it help with unwanted noise but also it helps the band stay on time and play in sync with one in another. Most bands that play with in-ear monitor systems have a metronome playing with each song. The metronome is like a "tick-tock" of a clock that keeps the band playing at the same tempo throughout the entire song. So while the band is playing and worshiping, in their ears they hear:

"tick tock, tick tock, tick tock, tick tock"

With this internal rhythm there's a standard set for them. This is your parameter. This is your order. This is your beat. It doesn't matter how many "white folk" are out there clapping off beat, or how many untamed tambourines are in the sanctuary, with the metronome the band is absolutely unfazed.

As believers who are *in pursuit*, we walk to a divine metronome of sorts. This is what Noah did. While everyone else was going crazy, losing their minds, living however they pleased, Noah was walking in sync with God and His plans for his generation.

The *assigning* mark of pursuit—speaks to the divine assignment that God has for our life. This assignment provides clarity and direction in a world of confusion and chaos.

There was a clear-cut distinction between the rhyme and rhythm of Noah's life, compared to the culture in which he was living. Noah was clapping on the 2 and the 4, and they were a hot mess on the 1 and the 3 (maybe!).

Why? Because he was on assignment! He couldn't afford to get caught up in the mess of his day and age, devoting all his time scrolling through social media getting distracted by the daily drama. He had work to do. He had an assignment to fulfill. He had an ark to build!

In this world in which we live, we are called to come out from the dysfunctional, chaotic, off-beat rhythm of our day and begin to focus in on a new beat. Let me put it like this: "Don't let Tommie Tambourine get you all in a funk. Push through the chaos and get in tune with the divine order of God's plan for your life."

IN PURSUIT!

The Apostle Paul put it like this,

> *And do not be conformed to this world, but be transformed by the renewing of your mind, that you may prove what is that good and acceptable and perfect will of God. (Romans 12:2)*

I like how *The Message* translates this verse, "Don't become so well-adjusted to your culture that you fit into it without even thinking."

What does it look like to be *in pursuit*? It means we march to a different beat than this world. It means we push through the distractions of our culture, and in the face of chaos and disorder, we align our passions and priorities to a different standard.

For individuals who are *in pursuit*, our passions and our priorities are not like the ones in our culture. We march to a different beat. We have a different assignment. And we do so UNASHAMEDLY, for we are *IN PURSUIT*.

You mean if I am going to be a person *in pursuit*, that I'm going to be different from the world in which I live?

YES. Absolutely. You are going to and should stand out from the day and hour in which you live. Just like Noah stood out from the culture in which he lived, so will those who are *in pursuit*.

COMING OF AGE

The writer of Hebrews said of Moses, "*By faith Moses, when he became of age, refused to be called the son of Pharaoh's daughter, choosing rather to suffer affliction with the people of God than to enjoy the passing pleasures of sin*" (Hebrews 11:24).

Stop for a moment and let this verse sink in. Let it get deep down in your spirit. Moses, when he became of age REFUSED to be CALLED the son of Pharaoh's daughter.

Interpretation:

> THE LIGHTS came on for MOSES, and he realized what HIS TRUE ASSIGNMENT was. He realized he didn't belong or "fit in" with the pattern or rhythm of the Egyptians.

He was different.

There was a divine calling on his life that was pulling on him, whispering in his ear, "You don't belong to Pharaoh." While every day he was surrounded and inundated by a culture which he was being told was "normal" and that he belonged to, something different was happening on the inside. He was hearing that divine metronome calling him to a different beat and rhythm than the one he was seeing and hearing. So what did Moses do?

He came of age and said, "I refuse to be called something I'm not."

"*In Pursuit*" is a calling out of the leaders of this generation. It is a cry for them to COME OF AGE. It's a cry to wake up and send a message to this world and to our culture: "I REFUSE TO BE CALLED YOUR

SON. I BELONG TO SOMEONE ELSE! I'm *in pursuit* of something DIFFERENT!"

It's a call for us to come of age—to grow up and come to our senses. This culture is not our home. It is not the end goal. It is not what we were created for. Too often we look to this trash heap as a trophy pile. Rather, God has called us out of this culture so that He can make us and shape us into what He has destined and purposed for our life.

I believe that today, even as you are reading these words on this page, the Spirit of God is stirring something in your heart. He is causing that *assigning* mark of pursuit to begin to burn inside of you. You realize you are tired of settling for the chaotic cadence of this culture, and you are ready to submit to God's divine assignment for your life. Let me remind you that nothing else in life will satisfy you other than the assignment God has for you.

After Peter experienced his devastating failure of denying Jesus, not once or twice, but three times, John's Gospel records Peter making an announcement to the other disciples, "I'm going fishing."

In this dark moment in Peter's life, with the shame and pain of his failure pressing in on him, Peter isn't expressing to his friends his need for some leisure time. Peter hasn't caught word around town that the fish are biting like crazy out at the sea of Galilee today. No, this isn't the case at all.

What Peter is saying in this moment is this: "I'm going back to my old life."

Where was Peter when Jesus called him to come and follow Him and become a disciple? He was at the lake.

Why?

Because he was a fisherman.

So in this moment in Peter's life, he's communicating to his friends, "I'm going back to my old life." He's essentially waving the white flag on God's assignment on his life.

Let me be crystal clear on this—this NEVER works out.

That night Peter and his disciple friends catch nothing—nada. Not one fish. Why? Because your life will always be empty, void, and incomplete apart from fulfilling God's direct assignment for your life. No matter how hard you try, no matter how good or gifted you think you are, a life *in pursuit* of anything but God's assignment will always leave your boat empty.

Not only will it leave you empty, but also in a mess. The story actually records that not only had Peter fished all night and caught nothing, but the next morning when Jesus calls out to Peter from the shore, Peter doesn't even have his clothes on! In this moment in time, let's be honest, Peter was a hot mess! He was tired, confused, frustrated, distraught, and the list goes on and on. This is how our plans leave us.

His order, his beat, his divine assignment is the only thing that will satisfy.

WHAT NOW?

So how do I start being *in pursuit* of God's assignment for my life? For a lot of people that in itself seems like an overwhelming concept, and they don't even know where to start.

A few years ago when I was on staff at my dad's church serving as his youth pastor, one of the things I had to do was to help him out in the baptismal tank when we baptized new believers.

I'll never forget one baptismal service as long as I live. One of our new converts who was going to be baptized happened to be a very "large" lady. I tell you with the utmost respect and sensitivity—this lady was BIG.

My dad was nervous. I had never seen him get like this before a baptism. I remember he actually pulled me in his office before service that night and said, "Now, son, you've got to really help me and pay attention when we baptize Sister (we'll just call her Jones) tonight."

I kind of just cracked a smile, to which he replied, "Now this is serious, son! We've got to make sure that we can get her back up out of the water!" I reassured him that we could do it.

Apparently my reassurance wasn't enough to satisfy his concerns, so he concocted a fairly brilliant plan. After all this wasn't his first rodeo. He later explained to the lady what the baptismal process would be like, and he mentioned that after he prayed, he would say the following words, "I now baptize you in the name of the Father, the Son, and the Holy Spirit." He then gave her some very *specific instructions*, "Immediately after I say, 'Holy Spirit,' I need you to squat. This is very important that you squat."

With her squatting, our job of getting her under the water would now be a little easier and hopefully we would still have enough leverage to get her back up.

BRILLIANT.

But, man, my pops was still nervous.

Then the moment of truth came. I don't remember how many we baptized that night to be honest with you, but I remember who was last. She was. As soon as she stepped in the water, my father tried to very discreetly get my attention. He gave me the kind of look that said, "You remember the plan, right?!?!?"

I winked back at him, letting him know I had his back. After a brief testimony, my dad began his prayer. I had heard my dad pray out loud for nearly 25 years of my life, but I had never heard him pray with such a nervous tone in his voice as he did that night in the tank.

When he finished his prayer, he said, "Sister Jones, upon your confession of faith in the Lord Jesus Christ, I now baptize you in the name of the Father, the name of the Son, and the name of the Holy Squat."

And that's the night we nearly lost someone in the tank—not because of their size but rather because I couldn't stop laughing!

You see my dad was so focused on how he was going to do this—baptize this lady and get her successfully back up out of the water—that he lost sight of the current step right in front of him.

The next step got ahead of the first step. And you know what they say, how do you baptize a big person? One step at a time!

But seriously, we do the same thing internally when we think about God's assignment for our life! We almost get overwhelmed by it to the point where we get so focused on what's next, or how am I going to get there, that we fail to just take one step at a time.

So here's the first step.

SURRENDER.

Let go and surrender to the *assigning* mark of *pursuit*.

Embrace the truth that God has a divine assignment for your life one that must be pursued!

Now is the TIME. Today is the day. Don't hold back. Don't worry about tomorrow or the next step. Today is the day to lay it on all the line and be *IN PURSUIT*.

CHAPTER 6

THE SHINING MARK OF PURSUIT

We are told to let our light shine, and if it does, we won't need to tell anybody it does. Lighthouses don't fire cannons to call attention to their shining—they just shine.

–D. L. Moody

A few years ago my wife and I went on a cruise with a group of about 30 other young ministers, who were all state or divisional youth directors in our church fellowship. One of the port cities on our cruise was the city of Progresso located in the Gulf of Mexico.

At this particular stop the majority of our group had decided against doing any specific on-shore excursions and had just decided to go check out the local destination and do some shopping. As we were strolling down the boardwalk with a few hundred other tourists, we were being bombarded by the locals trying to make some moolah before the ship departed. And when I say bombarded, I mean bombarded.

If you've ever been on a cruise you know exactly what I'm referring to.

We encountered one salesman who was really passionate about his job. You could hear his voice about 100 yards out. With every ounce of energy he had, he was trying to persuade customers in to his little seaside establishment for *<insert strong Mexican accent>* "De best margarrritas and tequila in Mehico."

As our group got closer he began to zero in on us. I'm sure he was thinking, *"Here's a nice size group of young 20-30 somethings on vacation—they look cool—hip—they're having a good time—this is gonna be a score—I can land this deal!"* Just from a quick glance, we were the pristine replica of what his target audience would be. He put on his best performance, and he tried absolutely everything to get us in his shop for some margaritas. We politely acknowledged him with a smile, said no thank you, and kept walking.

I'll never forget what happened next. As soon as we passed him, he stopped talking for a few seconds—the silence was actually eerie; he was obviously shocked he couldn't convince at least one of us to come in for a drink. Then, all of a sudden he turned around and said, "What's up with you guys? Are you guys Pentecostal or something?"

Now for the past two minutes walking down the boardwalk we hadn't stopped at all. But now we stopped dead in our tracks and started laughing hysterically! The reason we were laughing is because we actually were all Pentecostals—every last one of us.

Now, what tipped him off?

I can assure you it wasn't our hairstyles, or dress, but rather it was the fact that we had denied the alcohol. It was what we said "no" to.

If you grew up in church, or know anything about "church culture," you probably read the last chapter and first part of this one, and you're thinking, "I've heard this message before; I know what this is all about. All this talk about being different and not conforming. This is a call to 'Come out from among them And be separate' (2 Cor. 6:17), and to 'Be holy, for I am holy.' (1 Peter 5:16)."

You're probably thinking the same thoughts that salesman did in Progresso—I know exactly who these holy rollers are—I understand—I've met *holiness—pentecostal* people before, I know what this is all about.

But before you go all Progresso on me, let me stop you for a moment and allow me to point out something that makes a big difference about individuals who are "*in pursuit.*" Yes, while these commands of God's word (*come out, be separate, be holy, etc.*) are imperative for us to heed, that is only *part* of the beauty of what I want you to see from being "*in pursuit.*" Go with me for a moment here.

Let's take a quick look at Noah's life:

> *By faith, Noah built a ship in the middle of dry land. He was warned about something he couldn't see, and acted on what he was told. The result? His family was saved. **His <u>act of faith drew a sharp line</u> between the evil of the unbelieving world and the rightness of the believing world.** As a result, Noah became intimate with God.* (Hebrews 11:7, MSG)

What was it about Noah's life that "drew a sharp line" between the evil and chaos of his day and age and the "rightness" of the believing life?

Answer: His act of faith.

Let me translate it another way. Noah was known more for what he was for than for what he was against. He was known more for his YES, than his NO.

In the eyes and mind of that salesman in Progresso, he (along with much of our culture today) had equated a group of Christians (in this instance Pentecostals) with all of the things that they were against. I think I can make this broad statement, and for the most part it is fairly accurate:

> In today's culture, followers of Christ are often known more for *what we are against*, rather than *what we are for.*

This is something that I believe the Spirit of God is going to help us begin to change and shift. That is part of what *"in pursuit"* is all about.

I'm not saying that we shouldn't have standards and stand in opposition to certain things. Make no doubt we have to have absolutes in our life, and for sure we have to learn to take a stand in the face of a culture that is moving far away from God and the truth of His word. I'm not saying that we lose our spiritual backbones and don't have the guts to stand up for what we believe in. That's not what I'm saying at all. What I am saying, is that it's time to be known *more* for our acts of faith—for what we are doing—than for our voice of opposition.

In the midst of a dark and evil culture, Noah was known more for what he was for than for what he was against. It was his *act of faith* that drew the sharp, distinct line of difference between his life and the life of others. He was known for what he said YES to, and there was this extremely large boat in his backyard that gave proof of it!

Noah wasn't hanging around protesting the behaviors of his day. He wasn't slamming everyone for how screwed up they were or how ungodly their behaviors were. No, he was instead determined to be known for what he was about.

He was *in pursuit*.

Rather than having a sign in his hand that read something like, "turn or burn," "wrath is coming," "you're all going to die," instead he had a hammer in his hand and was building an ark of hope and deliverance. He was moving with godly fear and walking in obedience to what God had asked him to do, so that salvation could come to so many.

This is what people who are *"in pursuit"* are like. They are known more for their yes than their no. More for their pursuit than their protest.

Turn On The Lights

Paul wrote to the Church at Philippi and gave them this challenge:

Live clean, innocent lives as children of God, shining like bright lights in a world full of crooked and perverse people. (Philippians 2:15)

We live in a crooked, broken, and dark generation. However, in the middle of this chaos we have a very specific task—to shine! To stand out! To be *in pursuit!*

This is us.

This is our role.

This is our time to stand up and be *in pursuit.*

When we have priorities and passion aligned, and we are living in obedience to God's assignment for our life—our lives will begin to be the *"bright lights"* that Paul was writing about. People *"in pursuit"* are people of the light. They are continually shining by the life they live.

I love the way *The Message* version translates Proverbs 29:18, *"If people can't see what God is doing, they stumble all over themselves."*

I'm convinced that in our culture today, we don't have a darkness problem. We have a light problem. The problem is NOT that darkness is overtaking the light.

How do I know this?

Because light ALWAYS defeats darkness. Period.

Light has a spotless win record, completely undefeated. Light has never and will never be defeated.

Darkness has been defeated.

So the problem is we have a light problem. We're not shining! We've got to turn on the lights.

What we need is more Noahs, who are living their lives in such a way that their acts of faith and obedience speak so loud that it actually alters the course of history! It's time to let our lights shine.

Why is our culture "stumbling all over themselves"? Why are they so confused? So backward? So broken and desperate?

Answer: It's because they can't see what God is doing.

Interpretation: WE'VE GOT TO LET THEM SEE what it is like to be a follower of Christ. We've got to let our light shine. Somebody's got to turn the LIGHTS ON!

Instead of being so "turned off" at the wickedness and corruption of this world, people who are *in pursuit* take responsibility for their role in helping those who are stumbling all over themselves see the light of the incredible hope found in Jesus Christ! This was exactly what Jesus instructed us to do in Matthew 5:16, "*Let your light so shine before men, that they may see your good works and glorify your Father in heaven.*"

Every day that we drop our kids off for school, we speak a blessing over their lives before they get out of the vehicle. We've done this from their very first day of kindergarten, and our kids have come to expect it each day. The last part of that blessing is like a commissioning of sorts, and it simply goes like this, "*Love God, be a good leader, and let your light shine.*" You see I want my kids to know that each and every day that they are alive, they have a responsibility to let their light shine. It's the DNA of who we are as believers.

One day when my son got home from kindergarten, he seemed a little sad, so I asked him what was bothering him. He explained that he had been trying really hard to let his light shine at school and tell everyone about Jesus but it didn't seem to be working.

He went on to share with me that he had decided to start a club, and he called it the "Godly Children Club," but then he dropped his head and said, "But, Dad, I only have one other member besides me. Dad, nobody loves God in my school!"

After I comforted his little kindergarten heart, I told him how proud I was of him for letting his light shine at school. I explained to him that just because nobody wanted to be in his club didn't mean he wasn't making a difference at his school. I reminded him that all we have to do is just live our life as a Christian—love others, make good choices, etc.—and others would see our "light." Club, or no club—he would be making a difference.

As a dad, my heart was so full because my son was getting it! He understood that his life had purpose and that he had a responsibility to let his light shine. As followers of Christ *in pursuit*, we have a responsibility to the culture in which we live, and we must begin to take that responsibility seriously.

The next time you are in a major city and you get ready to cross a major intersection, or prepare to board a public transit vehicle, take note of the little yellow bumps on the ground. Most people, walk right over them and pay little to no attention to them and barely notice them—that is unless of course they are visually impaired or blind. These bumps are called "tactile paving"[1] or "truncated domes," and they serve as a ground surface indicator system, designed to alert those who are visually impaired of some type of approaching hazard.

Once felt with a walking cane or under foot, the visually impaired individual is made aware of approaching streets (traffic), hazardous surface, or grade changes. Essentially they are there as a warning to those who with their own eyes cannot see the potentially imminent danger they are about to walk "blindly" into.

As believers, *in pursuit*, this is us. This is our role. We are to be the "truncated domes" of our generation. They cannot see the imminent danger they are immersed in. They are lost—blinded to the truth—and as Proverbs says, "stumbling to the slaughter" (24:11), and it is absolutely imperative that we be the shining light that they need in this day and hour!

Be The Bridge

Charles Spurgeon said it best, "*Jesus DIED for sinners. Why can't we LIVE for them?*"

Some of us think, in regard to a lost friend or family member, "Man, if I could just get them to church." Here is the deal: YOU ARE THE CHURCH. We are the CHURCH. Take it to them with the life you live! Live your life *IN PURSUIT*.

The city of Choluteca is located in southern Honduras. The city sits on the Choluteca River and it serves as a major transit point along the Pan-American Highway. When Hurricane Mitch hit the region in 1998, it dumped 75 inches of rain in less than four days and absolutely devastated most of the country.

Amidst the destruction, 150 bridges were destroyed, but not the Choluteca bridge. After the storm passed and the flooding subsided, there the beautiful bridge stood in nearly perfect condition. An overhead view of the bridge however revealed that the roads on both sides of the bridge had completely vanished in the storm, with no trace of their previous existence. Even more remarkable, however, was the fact that during the massive flooding caused by the hurricane, the several-hundred-feet-wide Choluteca River had carved itself a new channel and now no longer flowed beneath the bridge at all. There the bridge stood spanning absolutely nothing but dry ground. This impressive structure quickly became known as "The Bridge to Nowhere."[2]

As the rebuilding began, some engineers suggested trying to redirect the massive Choluteca River back to flowing under the bridge. The idea was to try to reroute this massive body of water back to the bridge, rather than simply extending the bridge to where the river was now located.

As absurd as their idea sounded, too often this is our approach as believers with the lost. Rather than living out the gospel through our everyday lives and serving as the bridge of hope, we try to argue and fight over the best methods to get them to come to us.

People who are *in pursuit*, they are different.

They shine.

They live their assignment every day.

They have a relentless love for God and the things He loves.
Their life is that extension of hope to a lost and dying generation.
Let's be that hope.
Let's be that light.
Let's possess the shining mark of pursuit.

DECLA

P

THE RATION OF PURSUIT

INTRODUCTION

Now that we have discovered the concept of being *in pursuit* and taken a look at what that means, in the second part of this book I want us to take a look at just exactly *what* we should be *in pursuit* of. While section one was a *definition* of pursuit, section two is a *declaration* of pursuit.

I once read an amusing story told about Tommy Lasorda, the former manager of the LA Dodgers.

In the middle of a particular season where the Dodgers were really struggling to hit the ball, they had fallen deep into the bottom of the standings in the National League. One of the Dodgers scouts was out scouting in a podunk town in Nebraska when he stumbled upon something he thought was incredible.

The scout called Lasorda and said, "Tommy, I've just stumbled upon an amazing find; you won't believe this pitcher. This afternoon I just watched this kid throw a perfect game. Twenty-seven strikeouts in a row! Nobody was even close to touching the ball till a guy hit a foul in the ninth inning. So, Boss, the kid's with me right now, what do you think, shall I sign him up?"

"No," Lasorda replied, "sign up the guy who hit the foul ball . . . we need hitters."[1]

You see when it comes down to it, you've got to know what it is you need.

So now that we know what *in pursuit* means, we must discover *what* it is that we should be *in pursuit* of?

Paul, writing to his spiritual son Timothy, shares the following picture:

> *Flee also youthful lusts; but pursue righteousness, faith, love, peace with those who call on the Lord out of a pure heart.* (2 Timothy 2:22)

I love that Paul not only tells Timothy what to avoid, but more importantly he also tells him what to pursue. In essence, Timothy, my son, this is what you should be going after. This is what you should be pursuing. This is the journey you should be on.

While definitely not a comprehensive list, the second part of this book will cover some key areas that I feel are imperative that we be *in pursuit* of.

In Pursuit Of Purpose

If your Gospel isn't touching others through you, it hasn't truly touched You.

–Jeanne Mayo

I'll take the guy in the blue shirt.

Okay I'll take the tall dude.

I'll take him, the guy with glasses.

I'll take the redhead over there.

I'll take the little blonde girl; she's pretty fast.

. . . and so the dreaded "picking of the teams" continues.

Do you remember those playground day rituals? For many this brings back terrible memories—even just reading the conversation caused you to break out in a nervous sweat.

Will they pick me? Oh, no, please, Lord, don't let me be last, AGAIN. I know you said the first will be last and the last will be first—but I don't think you were referring to this game of pickup basketball—please, Lord!

Growing up, I typically didn't have problems getting picked up on a team, and as much as I'd like to attribute that to my plethora of athletic skills, it was more a result of my size. Every team can use an intimidator of sorts—and that was me—until the other team saw how tenderhearted

I was! Then the truth came out: I was merely a large, overcompetitive, teddy bear.

One of the things that we must be "*in pursuit*" of is our *purpose*.

Over the years, when I've been speaking to a crowd about *purpose* and the fact that God has a great plan for our lives, I couldn't help but begin to notice the look in some individuals' eyes.

On one occasion as I was talking about *purpose*, I could see that look in quite a few people's eyes, and it looked eerily familiar. I knew I had seen that look before. That nervous look of uncertainty. That look where you are trying to stay confident—strong—even convincing but inside you're a wreck. And then the light bulb went off, and I knew exactly where it came from.

THE PICKING OF THE TEAMS.

That was it.

It was that exact same look that was in everyone's eyes when the team captains began to choose teams. We so desperately want to play, we want a spot on the team, but we've done the math and realize only ten players are going to be chosen, and there're 15 of us in this line. And while we sit there trying to be strong and confident, there is something on the inside of us that is whispering, "You're gonna be sitting this one out."

This is what happens internally to so many people when we talk about *purpose*. Inside they're thinking, "Okay, this is exciting, God has an incredible plan for our lives and He has a purpose for us, but I know that the preacher—he's not talking about me—there's no way."

So we sit there, just like we did back on the playground, thinking there's no way the team captain is going to choose me.

But you see when God looks down on us, He doesn't say, "Okay, I'll take that one—and then that one—and then that one."

No, in fact God's picking of the team looks something like this: "Okay, I'll take all of y'all!" (Yes, I've added a Texas word to God's vocabulary.)

Every single one of us are chosen by God to fulfill His purposes and plans on the earth! Just listen to the words of Jesus recorded in John 15:16, "*You did not choose me, but I chose you.*" Let that sink in. Let that get deeply rooted into your heart and soul.

You were chosen.

You are chosen.

God has a purpose for your life, and it *must be pursued!"*

I love the MSG translation of 1 Peter 2:9-10:

> *But you are the ones chosen by God, chosen for the high calling of priestly work, chosen to be a holy people, God's instruments to do his work and speak out for him, to tell others of the night-and-day difference he made for you—from nothing to something, from rejected to accepted.*

Did you catch that? You are chosen to be God's instrument. He's called you. You are no longer a nothing, you are a something. You are no longer rejected, you are accepted. This, my friend, is divine!

You are on the team.

You are no longer sitting on the sidelines watching this thing unfold. NO, you are intricately woven into God's game plan! I like to say it like this: There is a divine call on your life, not a divine suggestion.

Jeremiah 1:5 says, "*Before I formed you in the womb I knew you, before you were born I set you apart; I appointed you as a prophet to the nations.*" Wow. Before we were even born, we were what? Set apart. We were chosen. We made the team. We were assigned a purpose!

I know what some of you are thinking right now: "Okay, that's cool that God chooses me, but when you talk about *calling* and *purpose* and being *used by God*, you are talking about people who are Pastors or Missionaries or Preachers—THOSE PEOPLE—not me."

WRONG.

I'm talking about you.

Yes, YOU. You have a divine purpose for your life—one that should get your attention, that should shake you, wake you, and cause you to begin to pursue it!

Yes, it is true that according to Ephesians 4:11, God calls or purposes for some to be "*apostles, some prophets, some evangelists, and some pastors and teachers,*" but that doesn't mean that's the end of the story and everyone else is off the team! The key is in the next part of that sentence: "*for the equipping of the saints for the work of ministry, for the edifying of the body of Christ.*"

Translation: Nobody's left out; we've all got a job to do!

I'll prove it to you. There's actually a real quick test you can take to determine whether or not God has a plan and purpose for your life. All you need is your cell phone.

Go ahead right now and pick up your cell phone, and I want you to hold it one inch from your mouth. Okay, are you ready for the big moment of truth? Now I want you to take a deep breath in and then deeply exhale.

Did your phone fog up? If so, then that means you are alive, and this, my friend, means that God has a purpose for your life!

One Expensive Car Wash

There's an Exxon Mobile station in Phoenix, Arizona, that will always be engraved deep in my memory. No, I didn't get gas for super cheap. And, no, as good as it sounds, I didn't have a killer hot dog or incredible slushy from this establishment either. It was nothing like that at all.

So why will I never forget this place? It's because I got a very expensive car wash there (and I mean VERY expensive).

It was almost midnight, and I was in the middle of conducting a week-long national youth event. Our team had just finished a successful concert night with a popular Christian artist, and we were making the final preparations for the next day of the event. We had already been at it now for a few days, and most of us were pretty exhausted at this point in the week. We finished helping the band load up and were finalizing the logistics for their early morning flight.

Due to some last-minute changes we had to make, I made the decision to load up all of the band's luggage and gear into a travel trailer and pull it with my SUV. Now instead of multiple drivers getting up in the middle of the night to make the trip to the airport, it could be done with one vehicle. I thought to myself, "This is a great solution. Thank God for travel trailers and large SUVS!"

And then I realized—wait a minute—I've just decided to shuttle the band in my SUV—mind you I have four young children who have been riding in that vehicle now for quite a few days on our long road trip. So off I went at around midnight to try to get my vehicle somewhat "presentable."

After scrounging for some quarters in the vehicle, I found a ghetto— spray it yourself—car wash with some vacuum cleaners, which is what I was really in need of. Fifteen minutes later the inside was pretty decent. I was impressed with myself. Then I thought, "You know, it wouldn't hurt to just wash the outside really quickly. You know you only get one chance to impress your special guests." The problem I encountered however, was that I was out of coins, and ghetto wash or whatever it was called didn't take credit cards.

So I made the quick decision to pull out my phone and google the closest gas station, where I planned to grab a soda and get some cash back for the car wash. I was relieved to see that right around the corner was a Circle K and I thought. "Man, this will be quick," and after a long day a giant Diet Mountain Dew sounded fantastic.

Right as I pulled up to the Circle K, I noticed across the street, the Exxon Mobil station and more importantly in big neon letters, "CAR

WASH" on their sign. Call it the lack of sleep, or low blood sugar, I don't know, but yet once again I called an audible and pulled into the Exxon Mobil station to take my car wash idea to the next level.

This was no do-it-yourself deal, this was a drive through, legit car wash, and I was so proud of myself and my audible capabilities (*Peyton Manning had NOTHING on me!*).

Now here is where my night rapidly changed.

Remember I mentioned that I had put all of the band's gear in a small travel trailer, and that trailer was attached to the back of my SUV? Mind you, I didn't forget about it being back there—I totally was aware of it—I just thought to myself, "You know what? I don't think this will be a problem at all." Now before you go calling me an idiot, it should be noted that this was a very, very small travel trailer—I mean it easily fit behind my SUV—no problem at all.

So I pulled up to the car wash, carefully read all of the signs, and I didn't see anything posted about not having any trailers on your vehicle or anything close to that verbiage. Still a little unsure, I took an extra step of caution and actually drove through the car wash first just to make sure everything looked okay with the trailer behind me.

After my test drive-thru, I swiped my card and entered the car wash. I pulled up until the light turned red and then I stopped and sat back to relax as the water started spraying over my car.

Next the soap came from the back and began to cover the vehicle; however, when it got to the front of my windshield, the soap sprayer came to an abrupt stop—leaving the rest of the front of the vehicle with no soap on it.

"That's odd," I thought to myself. And then absolutely nothing happened for like ten seconds. It was like the Car Wash was froze up or was re-buffering or something.

What happen next is what I'll never forget as long as I live.

All of a sudden the car wash came out of hibernation, and it did so in very violent fashion as the steel arm with the scrubbing brushes attached came hammering down on the back of my vehicle shattering through the hatchback.

No one will ever have to convince me how nice and quiet the inside of a GMC SUV is. I now know this personally because I realize how "airtight" the cabin is. And when it is that "airtight" and something (like a steel car wash arm) comes bursting through the glass it puts off quite the explosion!

I was dazed, confused, and honestly wasn't sure if this was really happening. I just sat there very numb for the next few minutes trying to pull myself back together!

Needless to say, after it was all said and done, I ended up with ONE EXPENSIVE CAR WASH.

Likewise, when I talk about the fact that God has a purpose for every life, and one that is to be pursued, you must realize that purpose didn't come cheap. Make no mistake about it, your purpose has a price tag! Paul explained it this way, "*For you were bought at a price; therefore glorify God in your body and in your spirit, which are God's*" (1 Corinthians 6:19-20).

It is imperative that even as you read these words that you understand that not only is there a purpose for your life, but God paid dearly for that purpose.

You were bought at a price.

God has invested dearly in you and He has a purpose for your life. Paul explained it this way a few chapters later in 2 Corinthians 4:7, "*We have this treasure in earthly vessels. . . .*" The purpose of God that resides in your life, which was deposited by God, is like a treasure, a special deposit—one that we must do something with. We must PURSUE IT.

You must be *in pursuit* of purpose!

Holy Homework

With four kids in our house, it seems like somebody is always needing some help with their homework. As the kids get older, I admit, this gets both more challenging and humbling. Thank God for Google and lightning fast i-phones. Thanks to both of these, all a parent needs is a good ten-second distraction and, BOOM, of course your parents know how to do this problem—piece of cake!

When the kids were in kindergarten everything was a lot simpler. Math for example was a breeze. Everything was on flash cards.

$$2 + 2 = (flip\ the\ card\ over)\ 4$$
$$3 + 2 = (flip\ the\ card\ over)\ 5$$

Simple, easy.

In this dark world that we live in, God has a plan and a purpose. He's not caught off guard by the wickedness of this day and age. All the evil and hatred haven't worn Him down and thrown off His plan—NO, not at all.

God still has a plan, and the exciting part is that in that divine plan *He chooses to use you and me!*

In fact, would you like to take a sneak peek at God's flash card for the world in which we live? Here it is:

Christ + You = Hope

Colossians 1:27 says, "*Christ in you, the hope of glory.*" Why is it imperative that we be *in pursuit* of purpose? Because we are a part of God's plan for humanity! Just like Noah who said "Yes" to the purpose of God for his generation, the call still goes out today for those who will stand up and be *in pursuit* of their purpose.

Our world is counting on it.

The lost are counting on it.

Counting on what?

Christ in you! They need the hope that has been invested in you. Bill Hybels says it like this, "The local church is the hope of the world."

Hope will not come from the next economic boom or presidential candidate or from anywhere else. It will come from God's original game plan found in Matthew 16:18, "*I will build my church, and all the powers of hell will not conquer it*" (NLT).

So how about it friend?

What do you say?

Are you ready to team up with the long line of radical followers of Christ who have completely abandoned themselves *in pursuit* of God's purpose for their life? The culture we live in today will not be won over or changed by the mildly interested. This is not a day and hour for the faint of heart. We must be *in pursuit*.

I say, let's move in that direction, let's be *in pursuit* of purpose.

Let me end this chapter with the poem "Only One Life," penned by missionary C. T. Studd born on December 2, 1860. This poem encompasses one who is *in pursuit* of purpose:

Two little lines I heard one day,
Traveling along life's busy way;
Bringing conviction to my heart,
And from my mind would not depart;
Only one life, 'twill soon be past,
Only what's done for Christ will last.

Only one life, yes, only one,
Soon will its fleeting hours be done;
Then, in 'that day' my Lord to meet,
And stand before His Judgement seat;
Only one life, 'twill soon be past,
Only what's done for Christ will last.

Only one life, the still small voice
Gently pleads for a better choice
Bidding me selfish aims to leave,
And to God's holy will to cleave;
Only one life, 'twill soon be past,
Only what's done for Christ will last.

Only one life, a few brief years,
Each with its burdens, hopes, and fears;
Each with its days I must fulfill,
Living for self or in His will;
Only one life, 'twill soon be past,
Only what's done for Christ will last.

When this bright world would tempt me sore,
When Satan would a victory score;
When self would seek to have its way,
Then help me, Lord, with joy to say;
Only one life, 'twill soon be past,
Only what's done for Christ will last.

Give me, Father, a purpose deep,
In joy or sorrow Thy word to keep;
Faithful and true what e'er the strife,

Pleasing Thee in my daily life;
Only one life, 'twill soon be past,
Only what's done for Christ will last.

Oh, let my love with fervor burn,
And from the world now let me turn;
Living for Thee, and Thee alone,
Bringing Thee pleasure on Thy throne;
Only one life, 'twill soon be past,
Only what's done for Christ will last.

Only one life, yes, only one,
Now let me say, "Thy will be done";
And when at last I'll hear the call,
I know I'll say "'Twas worth it all";
Only one life, 'twill soon be past,
Only what's done for Christ will last.[1]

IN PURSUIT OF PRESENCE

Practice the presence of God.

–Brother Lawrence

"Will they repeat the chorus or go back to verse one?"

"Maybe they'll go to the bridge?"

"Or maybe the Spirit will lead them to sing verse one again for the tenth time . . ."

These were the thoughts that raced through my mind as I listened closely to the worship team, focused intently on their every move. I clutched the next two transparency sheets (*verse one and the bridge*) firmly in my right hand (*trying not to smear the handwritten ink*), while my left hand was strategically positioned three inches from the projector and I was ready to make my move.

Whichever direction the worship leader was headed next, I was poised and ready to make the switch. I was the fastest transparency switcher east of the Mississippi, or at least I thought I was, and I wasn't about to screw this up.

This was most of my early childhood years as a PK in church, switching out those good ol' transparencies. It was the early '90s, the worship "transition" was in full effect, and our church was somewhere in between page 121 of the red backs and *"He Has Made Me Glad."*

I laugh as I think back about all the times I sorted through all those transparency sheets, wrote out new choruses, and even on more than one occasion put the transparencies on upside down (*Complete accident, honestly, Dad, I promise*).

Somewhere, back in those childhood days of mine as I swapped out the transparencies in our worship services, something was deposited deep down in my heart—something that has forever impacted my life.

I'm not sure if it was the lyrics that I consistently read over and over again that dug deep down into my spirit, or if it was the passionate worship of our congregation that I was submersed in—or perhaps a little bit of both—regardless of what is was, *something* changed in me.

That *something*, was the birth of a deep desire for the presence of God. I'm talking about a desire that absolutely nothing but the presence of God can fulfill.

A passion for His presence.

A passion like the psalmist had who proclaimed in Psalm 84:10:

> *"Better is one day in your courts than a thousand elsewhere; I would rather be a doorkeeper in the house of my God than dwell in the tents of the wicked."*

Once you've truly experienced the presence of God, there is nothing in this world that can compare to it.

One of the things that we must be *"in pursuit"* of is *presence*. The living, tangible, real, genuine presence of God. The presence that changes you in an instant, the presence that satisfies the deepest longing of your heart. The presence that makes you join with the psalmist and proclaim, *"My soul yearns, even faints, for the courts of the LORD; my heart and my flesh cry out for the living God"* (Psalm 84:2).

As you read through the book of Psalms, you can't help but feel the passion expressed for the presence of God.

As the deer longs for streams of water, so I long for you, O God. I thirst for God, the living God. When can I go and stand before him? (Psalm 42:1-2, NLT)

Make no mistake about it, the psalmists were *in pursuit* of the presence of God.

I believe with all my heart that in this day and hour God is wanting to reawaken inside of our hearts a *pursuit of presence*.

MAKE SPACE

I love reading through the book of Joshua in the Old Testament. I'm fascinated in so many ways as I read this historical book. What intrigues me the most is trying to imagine how Joshua must have felt as he began to lead the children of Israel after Moses passed away.

Talk about big shoes to fill. Wow.

Sure, the children of Israel were out of Egyptian bondage, through the Red Sea, and headed to the promised land, but now they've been some forty years in the wilderness and the promises of the land flowing with milk and honey seem like a fading memory.

I'm sure Joshua had to be overwhelmed. I'm sure somewhere along the line he had to think to himself, "Man, if Moses couldn't do this thing, how in the world am I going to? What happens if they turn on me like they started to turn on Moses? Will we really be able to defeat the giants that are in the land?" But yet scripture doesn't record any nervous breakdowns with this steady leader, just a rock solid resolve to move forward and lead God's people into the promised land.

I wonder what gave Joshua such a peace? Such a confidence? Such a boldness to lead God's people into uncharted territory?

I believe the secret is revealed in Exodus chapter 33:

> *⁷Moses took his tent and pitched it outside the camp, far from the camp, and called it the tabernacle of meeting. And it came to pass that everyone who sought the LORD went out to the tabernacle of meeting which was outside the camp. ⁸So it was, whenever Moses went out to the tabernacle, that all the people rose, and each man stood at his tent door and watched Moses until he had gone into the tabernacle. ⁹And it came to pass, when Moses entered the tabernacle, that the pillar of cloud descended and stood at the door of the tabernacle, and the LORD talked with Moses. ¹⁰All the people saw the pillar of cloud standing at the tabernacle door, and all the people rose and worshiped, each man in his tent door. ¹¹So the Lord spoke to Moses face to face, as a man speaks to his friend.*
> (Exodus 33:7-11)

Moses would go out to the tabernacle of meeting, and there he would meet with the Lord. When he would enter the tabernacle, scripture records that the cloud would descend—this is representative of the presence of the Lord. So in essence Moses would go out and be in *the presence* of the Lord, where he would meet face to face with the Lord.

I don't know about you, but in my mind this is pretty incredible!

As amazing as it is that Moses would go out and pursue the presence and meet face to face with God, to me, that isn't even the most remarkable part of the story. Check out how the passage ends:

> *And he (Moses) would return to the camp, **but his servant Joshua the son of Nun, a young man, did not depart from the tabernacle**.* (vs. 11)

Here we see what I believe is the epicenter of Joshua's life and leadership—it is his foundation. Joshua was passionate about the presence. He lingered in the presence. He didn't want to leave. When Moses left, he stayed.

I can imagine Joshua saying, "Come on, Moses, just a few more minutes. One more song! Just a few more moments of solemn adoration. I don't want to leave this place!"

I believe that it was in these holy moments where a great hunger and desire was birthed inside of this young leader for the presence of God. This pursuit for the presence would carry over into Joshua's legacy as he began to lead the Children of Israel.

Immediately after Joshua takes over the leadership role, he stands ready to lead the children of Israel through the Jordan river and to begin to enter the promised land. So here Joshua stands—first few days on the job—and let's take note of the instructions that his leaders/commanders give the children of Israel.

> *When you see the ark of the covenant of the LORD your God, and the priests, the Levites, bearing it, then you shall set out from your place and go after it. (Joshua 3:3)*

So Joshua's leaders, influenced and led by Joshua, instruct the Israelites that when they see the ark of the covenant (which represents the presence of God), they are to GO AFTER IT.

Translation: Pursue the presence!

You can see the hunger, desire, and priority of the presence that Joshua had now flowing through every fabric of his leadership.

GO AFTER IT!

The instructions continue:

> *Yet there shall be **a space** between you and it, about two thousand cubits by measure. Do not come near it, that you may know the way by which you must go, for you have not passed this way before.* (vs. 4)

I absolutely love this part of the instructions. Let me help translate it:

When you see the presence, make space for it. I'm taking you to places—levels—that you've never been before and you NEED THE PRESENCE! Make space for it. Don't get ahead of it. Don't get so busy in all your pursuits that you forget to MAKE SPACE for the ultimate pursuit of His presence!

Joshua made space.

He was *in pursuit* of presence.

DISCONNECTED

Of course it's nearly impossible to talk about pursuing God's presence without mentioning David. David was the epitome of someone who was *in pursuit* of presence. He penned Psalm 63, perhaps one of the most famous passages regarding the presence of God:

> *O God, You are my God;*
> *Early will I seek You;*
> *My soul thirsts for You;*
> *My flesh longs for You*
> *In a dry and thirsty land*
> *Where there is no water.*
> *So I have looked for You in the sanctuary,*
> *To see Your power and Your glory.* (vs. 1-2)

David understood the priority of God's presence, and he was obsessed with pouring his heart out in passionate praise and adoration. I believe it was David's love, admiration, and esteem for God's presence that was one of the main reasons that God said the following about David:

> *I have found David the son of Jesse, a man after My own heart, who will do all My will.* (Acts 18:22)

I believe David's pursuit of God's presence is what developed and made him into a man after God's own heart! The good news is that we can position ourselves in the same direction. Like David, we can get connected to the Father-heart of God and live in such unity and intimacy with the presence of God beyond anything we could ever imagine. How?

By pursuing the presence of God.

A few years ago, I opened one of the greatest birthday gifts I've ever received. I should point out that I absolutely LOVE to open presents— and I like to receive lots of them! On this particular birthday when I ripped open my gift to find an Apple watch, I nearly lost my mind. I couldn't believe this was really happening. The Apple watches had just come out, and those who know me well know that I'm a huge Apple fan. I had been drooling over the watches ever since they came out, and in this moment, I stood there in disbelief that I finally had one.

The next few weeks I was in technology heaven. My new watch could do all kinds of cool things. Every few minutes it was buzzing on my wrist—notifying me of important events or calls or texts. I felt connected like never before.

Now every time someone called or texted, I didn't have to dig my iPhone out of my pocket; with a few flicks of my finger on my watch I could respond and move on. Winner, winner, chicken dinner!

But about one month in something happened. One day I noticed that my phone rang and my watch didn't do anything—no ping—vibration, etc. So after I hung up the phone, I looked down at my watch to see what was up. Then I saw that my watch was "locked out." The lock feature on the watch kicks in any time the watch is removed from your wrist—essentially keeping anyone else from accessing your watch without a password.

"This is odd," I thought. "I don't remember taking my watch off. I wonder how it got locked out?" I quickly just punched in the password and went on. A few minutes later I glanced down at my wrist to check the time and, lo and behold, my watch was locked out AGAIN. I was puzzled.

To make a long story short, after multiple phone calls and trips to the Apple store, it was determined that my watch had become defective.

The problem? The sensors in the watch that determined whether or not my watch was on my wrist had gone bad. As a result my watch would always stay locked out. Never in sync, never in rhythm, never functioning the way it was intended.

Likewise the same happens to us spiritually when we fail to *pursue* God's presence. We get locked out and out of sync with the Father-heart of God. When we fail to make space for, prioritize, and pursue God's presence, we become just like my first Apple watch—we live way below the God-given potential that we have.

I don't know about you, but I want to make space for the presence. I want to linger like Joshua did. I want to desire it like David did.

With everything that pulls on our time, attention, and energy, I want to heed the advice of Solomon when he penned, "Do not be in a hurry to leave the king's presence" (Ecclesiastes 8:3, NIV).

Amen.

So be it.

Let's be *in pursuit* of presence.

In Pursuit Of Prayer

You are only ONE PRAYER away from a totally different life.

–Mark Batterson

When the 38 members of the Green Bay Packers football team reported for training camp in July of 1961, they were ready to move forward into a brand new season. The last season had ended on a sour note as the Pack suffered a heartbreaking loss to the Philadelphia Eagles, squandering a fourth-quarter lead in the NFL Championship game.

The off-season had been long, and as the team gathered, they were eager to put this brutal loss behind them and move on. They were ready to take their game to the next level and start working on the details and game plans that would help them win a championship.

Their coach, a man by the name of Vince Lombardi, came in that morning with a different idea, and started off training camp in a way that was quite surprising to these professional football players.

"This is a football."

In the book *When Pride Still Mattered: A Life of Vince Lombardi* author David Maraniss explains what happened when Lombardi walked into training camp on that day in the summer of 1961.

He took nothing for granted. He began a tradition of starting from scratch, assuming that the players were blank slates who carried over no knowledge from the year before. . . . He began with the most elemental statement of all. "Gentlemen," he said, holding a pigskin in his right hand, "this is a football."[1]

Mind you, Lombardi wasn't coaching a group of rookies, or peewee pig skinners here; he was coaching professional athletes, athletes who just a few months prior had come oh so close to winning the biggest prize their sport could offer. But where did he start? He started at the very beginning. The basics.

Lombardi's coaching approach of the fundamentals continued all throughout training camp. Each player reviewed even the basic fundamentals of how to block and tackle. The team went back to page one on the playbook and went from there. Lombardi was obsessed with returning to the basics.

The result? His team would become the best in the league at the tasks everyone else took for granted, and six months later the Green Bay Packers would defeat the New York Giants 37-0 to win the NFL Championship.

This however, was only the start. Lombardi went on to become one of the greatest football coaches of all time. He would never lose in the playoffs again. In total, Lombardi would go on to win five NFL Championships in a span of seven years, including three in a row.

He never coached a team with a losing record.

Why?

He went back to the basics—the fundamentals.

I know this will sound very basic what I'm about to say, but I'm going to say it anyway:

We need to be *in pursuit* of prayer.

Prayer is a fundamental that we must get back to. It doesn't sound real flashy, and it seems rather simple, almost elementary, but prayer is something that we must be *in pursuit* of.

One of my absolute favorite scriptures is recorded in Luke 5:16, which says of Jesus, "*So He Himself often withdrew into the wilderness and prayed.*" This verse intrigues me. It inspires me. It reminds me of the story of Lombardi standing in front of his team, saying, "This is a football." Here we have Jesus, the very son of God—absolutely 100% perfect—who, scripture records, *often* withdraws to secluded places to do what? PRAY.

Back to the basics.

The fundamentals.

Jesus paints a beautiful picture for us on the importance of prayer. He reminds us of the priority and necessity of personal communion with God through the intimacy of prayer. Prayer is something that we must be *in pursuit* of. Jesus said in Matthew 6:6, "*But when you pray, go into your room, close the door and pray to your Father*" (NIV). I love these simple but profound instructions Jesus gives us on prayer.

Close the door.

A simple instruction, right? But stop and think about it, let it sink in.

Close the door, remove all the other distractions. The KRV (King Randy Version) says, "*But when you pray, go into your room, turn off your iPhone, and pray to your Father.*" Whatever adjustments must be made, make them! Embrace the moments of just you and the Lord. Don't run from it. Don't be ashamed of it. Embrace it. Shut the door and be *in pursuit* of prayer!

This must become a priority for us. I love what Jeanne Mayo says of prayer, "*If we honor God with our time, He will honor us with His voice.*" I don't know about you but I want to hear His voice. I want to know His voice and obey it.

Our world right now needs men and women who know how to get in touch with God and receive a word from heaven. However, in order for this to happen we must be closing the door and embracing prayer.

Judges chapter 6 records the following, "*And it came to pass, when the children of Israel cried out to the Lord because of the Midianites (the enemy), that the Lord sent a prophet.*"

Translation for today: There are a lot of people held in bondage by the enemy, and we need prophets with a WORD! I'm not talking about a nice message downloaded from the internet with, three points, a joke, and a poem, but a true word from the LORD. And this, my friend, will only come from one place, the *secret place of prayer*.

The 19th-century missionary and revivalist Andrew Murray said, "O, let the place of secret prayer become to me the most beloved spot on earth." May this again become our earnest desire! May the secret place no longer be a neglected place but a treasured place.

Psalm 25:14, says, "*The secret of the Lord is with those who fear Him.*" I believe with all my heart that if we will return to the pursuit of prayer, of humbling ourselves, closing the door—which shows honor, reverence and respect to the Lord—that He will begin to share His secrets with us.

A closed door will eventually lead to an open heaven.

The Altar Of Prayer

I think the church in America (generally speaking) has lost sight of the value or importance of prayer. Corrie ten Boom used to ask, "Is prayer your steering wheel or your spare tire?" I think most would agree that all too often we've viewed it as our spare tire.

I hope that you don't take offense, misunderstand, or take out of context what I'm about to say. Those who know me well know that I love to do things with a spirit of excellence. I love to plan, to practice, and to execute things well. For instance, when I am leading a church service, I like to have a sense of order, structure, and flow. I like to plan the service out and do everything in the most excellent way possible. However, with that said, there used to be a day in the church when leaders would gather early before service to do one thing:

To pray.

And when I say pray, I mean pray. This wasn't your 30-second gathering in a quick huddle type of prayer, they came to pray, intercede on behalf of the souls of men who would gather in the service. Long before most of the congregation would arrive, leaders would kneel and bombard heaven on behalf of the service about to take place.

They came early to pray.

Today, we gather early to rehearse.

Again, before you throw this book out of your hand, understand me: I'm not knocking rehearsals, service run-throughs, or diligent planning. I think those items are of a high value and in fact I wish we did more of it in many of our circles today. But what I am saying is, what would happen if we did both? What would happen if we *planned* AND *prayed*? If we *rehearsed* AND *repented*. If we *knew* AND we *knelt*. Like Mark Batterson says, "Pray like it DEPENDS ON GOD and work like it DEPENDS ON YOU."

Again, it doesn't have to be an either/or, it can be both. We need both. But make no mistake about it, we have to return to the place where we value the importance of prayer.

Jesus said that His house should be called what? A house of prayer (Matthew 21:13). For many churches today I think the title that is more fitting is a house of production. We've placed much more emphasis on a *production chart* than we have on *our Father who art*. I believe the world has yet to see what would happen if a group of believers or leaders would not only have a passion for excellence but also a passion for prayer.

In his book, *Why Revival Tarries*, Leonard Ravenhill shares the following powerful thoughts on prayer:

No man is greater than his prayer life. The pastor who is not praying is playing; the people who are not praying are straying. The pulpit can be a shop window to display one's talents; the prayer closet allows no showing off.

Poverty-stricken as the Church is today in many things, she is most stricken here, in the place of prayer. We have many organizers, but few agonizers; many players and payers, few pray-ers; many singers, few clingers; lots of pastors, few wrestlers; many fears, few tears; much fashion, little passion; many interferers, few intercessors; many writers, but few fighters. Failing here, we fail everywhere.[2]

I believe the Lord wants to raise up modern day Elijah's of whom scripture records in 1 Kings 18:30, "*And he (Elijah) repaired the altar of the Lord that was broken down.*" Notice in this familiar Old Testament story, that before fire ever comes down from heaven, before the enemy is defeated and the drought is over with rain from heaven—before all of these miracles—the altars are rebuilt.

Dear friend, let's return to and rebuild the altar of prayer, both personally and corporately! It's time to be *in pursuit* of prayer.

I love what multiple accounts record of William Seymour during the Azusa Street Revival. The pulpit at the meeting place on Bonnie Brae Street was composed of two large wooden "shoe boxes." Here Seymour would usually sit behind these boxes, deep in prayer with his head buried inside the top box. Seymour lay prostrate and broken before the Lord in prayer as God poured out his Spirit. He pursued the Lord in prayer, and the Lord responded and our world has never been the same.

In Psalm 50, the Lord brings some powerful charges against His people. I absolutely love the "straight talk" that the Lord has with His people:

O my people, listen as I speak, Here are my charges against you, O Israel: I am God, your God! I have no complaint about your sacrifices or the burnt offerings you constantly bring to my altar. But I want no more bulls from your barns; I want no more goats from your pens. (Psalm 50:7-9, NLT)

I love how the Lord tippy-toes around the issue at hand. NOT! The message is clear. I don't want any more of your bulls! I don't want any more of your goats! Stop playing around here! You're just going through the religious routine, and you're missing the point.

My translation, and please pardon the pun: "Excuse me here folks, but your bull is just that, it's bull. Let's get to the heart of the issue here."

What the Lord was looking for was something that was *real* and *genuine*. The Lord goes on to say, "What I want instead is your true thanks to God; I want you to fulfill your vows to the Most High." (vs 14). He wanted authentic, genuine thanksgiving. He wanted the vows to be real. The sacrifices to be right. As David declared, "*The sacrifice you desire is a broken spirit. You will not reject a broken and repentant heart, O God.*" (Psalm 51:17, NLT).

Oh, how easy it is for our prayer life to turn into these religious routines. Here's what I'm supposed to say, here's what I'm supposed to do. Check this off, check that off, rather than coming humbly and broken before the Lord with the sacrifice of a contrite heart. What we want is a rending of our hearts and not our garments (Joel 2:13). It's the inner work rather than just the outer appearance.

Ask yourself, is my prayer life *routine* or is it *real*?

Am I *faking* it, or *fostering* it?

One day, one of Jesus' disciples made a simple request on behalf of the disciples, "*Teach us to pray*" (Luke 11:1). Have you ever read that and thought, "Man, I thought these guys knew how to pray—I mean after all they are the disciples—don't they know all about prayer?" But notice Jesus doesn't condemn him or the others for the inquiry. No, in fact I think it brought great joy to Him. Perhaps He thought, "Yes! They are getting it! They want to learn how to pray, how to commune with my Father."

I don't know about you, dear friend, but I don't want to act like I know everything about prayer. I want to know more about the wonderful privilege that Jesus paid for in allowing me to come before the throne of grace. I want to be *in pursuit* of it. I want to discover it. I want to tap in to all that is available through the privilege I have to come before God in prayer.

The Java Master

There are a few things I remember about riding in the car with my dad as a child.

First, I was always amazed and mesmerized to watch his cup of coffee just sit on the dashboard while he drove—without spilling. And I'm not talking about a travel mug. This was years before Yeti's and fancy Starbucks mugs. This was just a plain ol' ceramic coffee cup with no lid. It would just magically sit there on the dashboard full of coffee without spilling. Now I admit I am prone to being distracted by shiny objects, however, even now as an adult looking back, this feat was and still is utterly amazing to me!

The second thing I remember about car rides with my father, was just how honestly bad of a driver my dad was (this point makes my first memory even more incredible). The last thing I recall is that I never remember riding in a vehicle with my dad, where at some point during the trip I couldn't distinctly hear a soft, gentle, yet passionate sound coming from him. On the way to school, to the ball game, to the store, family vacations, on and on and on—it didn't matter—at some time or another it was there.

It wasn't loud.

It wasn't obnoxious.

In fact you couldn't even see his lips moving, but you knew it was happening.

It wasn't until later on in life, that I discovered what that was; It was the sound of my dad praying in the Spirit.

First Thessalonians 5:17, simply says: *"Pray without ceasing."* I love the definition of this term "without ceasing" in the Greek, as it implies *"without intermission."* Yes, I am a firm believer that we need to have our set time and place of prayer. We need to have those times when we go into the room and close the door. We must establish this discipline in our personal lives. However, we also cannot forget about the discipline of *praying without intermission!* Too often our goal in our prayer times is to get to the "Amen," and we look at that as our finish line. What I'm suggesting is that, rather than a finish line or a period at the end of a sentence, may our "Amens" serve as a catalyst to a lifestyle of prayer "without intermission."

May we be *in pursuit* of prayer without ceasing!

In the car, at the office, standing in line at the grocery store, there are no limits to our prayer life unless we choose to set them!

I now realize looking back on life, many of those soft, gentle sounds were deep prayers for me that I know have saved my life from destruction countless times over. I hope that, now as a Father of four children myself, I can model this life of "prayer without intermission" to them.

Now the coffee cup trick? I'll leave that one to my pops; I'm quite content with the lid on my Yeti.

Let's leave the lid on the coffee mug and take the lid off of our prayer life; it's time to be *in pursuit* of prayer.

IN PURSUIT OF PURITY

The proof of spiritual maturity is not how pure you are but awareness of your impurity. That very awareness opens the door to grace.

–Philip Yancey

One of my favorite things to do on Saturday mornings when our family happens to be home, is to get up and cook breakfast for the kids. There's just something about dad cooking breakfast that really seems to excite the kids, and I actually really look forward to it. It's become "one of our things" as a family.

On one such occasion, I was up fairly early, so I headed to the kitchen to get started. I asked the kids what they would like, and they requested one of their favorites: biscuits with chocolate gravy. Now if you didn't have the privilege of growing up in the south, you probably don't know what biscuits and chocolate gravy are—and you might even be thinking how terrible that sounds. My southern friends on the other hand, they know all about this nice little delicacy.

After going through all the hard work of opening the canned biscuits and putting them in the oven (move over Martha Stewart), I turned to the fun part, making the chocolate gravy. I set out all the ingredients and had everything ready to start the gravy about 5-10 minutes before the biscuits would be finished. As I started working on the gravy, everything was going just as planned until I added the flour. After adding the flour I began to whisk the gravy just like I always do, however on this morning the gravy didn't seem to be thickening up like normal. I naturally thought I just needed a little more flour so I added it and kept on whisking.

Still nothing.

Once again I added just a little bit more—still no change.

At this point I was getting a little frustrated. My next thought was that maybe I wasn't whisking fast enough. So I really kicked it into high gear and was whisking like a mad man!

It was at this point that my wife enters the kitchen for the first time. It was either the sweat coming off my forehead, the anxiety in my face, or the furious whisking that tipped her off that my little daddy's diner was having some issues.

She calmly asked, "What's wrong sweetheart?"

To which I looked up and said, "I can't get this stinking gravy to thicken up! I keep adding flour and nothing is happening!!!"

She examines the situation for a brief second, then proceeds to pick up my "flour" container and says, "How many times have I told you this ISN'T flour. This, is POWDERED SUGAR."

Needless to say, my chocolate gravy that day was off the charts and the kids absolutely loved it!

Jesus, speaking to believers in Matthew 5:13, said, *"You are the salt of the earth."* I love the comparison that He makes between our lives as believers and salt. Salt has a very specific purpose, which we as believers must have as well.

Salt is a preservative.

Salt is for seasoning.

Salt is a purifying agent.

Jesus finishes the thought by saying, "*but if the salt loses its flavor, how shall it be seasoned?*" In other words, Jesus is saying you've got to make sure you don't lose your flavor, don't lose your saltiness, your purpose.

You see sometimes we've got to take time to *double check the ingredients* to make sure we are cooking with the right stuff!

I love how THE MSG translation records the same verse:

> *Let me tell you why you are here. You're here to be salt-seasoning that brings out the God-flavors of this earth. If you lose your saltiness, how will people taste godliness? You've lost your usefulness and will end up in the garbage.*

Sometimes we think we are "salty" but we're not. We've got to learn to double check the ingredients. We think we've got it, but upon closer examination we discover that something is off. I believe that today, more than ever before, this can be said about one aspect of the believer's life not being salty enough; that aspect is our *purity*.

Proverbs 30:12 (NKJV) says, "*There is a generation that is pure in its own eyes, Yet is not washed from its filthiness.*" Translation: Sometimes we think we are pure, but in all reality we are quite the opposite. Sometime we think we've got everything under control, but upon closer examination there is some chaos in the kitchen!

Purity.

I believe one of the things we must be *in pursuit* of is purity. It must become a priority for us, something that we understand and are *in pursuit* of.

Jesus said in Matthew 5:8, "*Blessed are the pure in heart, For they shall see God.*" If we want to see God do great things in our midst, to see him move like never before in our lives, then we must return to what?

A pure heart.

I don't know about you, but I want to see God. I want to see Him manifest His power and glory. I want to see His Spirit poured out on all flesh. I want to see God do exceedingly abundantly above all we could ever ask or imagine, but where does it start?

It starts with a pure heart.

THIS ISN'T PRESCHOOL ANYMORE

My youngest daughter is named Cali Grace. We gave her the beautiful middle name of "Grace" thinking, "Surely she'll come out and live up to her name." What we've discovered is that our name choice has turned more into the realization of how much "Grace" we've needed as parents in raising her.

One day not too long ago when she was in kindergarten, I got home from work and she immediately called me into her room for something very important. I came in and she closed the door. I knew this was serious, the type of 5-year-old, kindergarten serious.

I asked her what was going on, to which she replied, "Dad, today at school I had to change my color." This is kindergarten code talk for, "I got in trouble."

"Okay," I said, "so tell me what happened?"

She took a deep breath and told me about her day, "Well, you see, Dad, we were out at the playground for recess, and this boy in my class, he totally pooped his pants! It was so gross! When he did, I looked at him and said: *What do you think this is, preschool?*"

That was it for me, I immediately burst into laughter!

After I composed myself, realizing that someone had to be the adult in the room, I pointed out to Cali how maybe she could make a better choice of words when confronting her friend, and how he was probably really embarrassed. She agreed and showed me that she was already working on an apology letter for her friend.

After leaving the room, it hit me: We need more friends in our life like Cali. Friends who will be brutally honest with us and confront us in the areas of our life where we are drastically underperforming! Friends who will say, "Come on this isn't preschool anymore. You can't be pooping your pants on the playground! This is kindergarten! Grow up!"

I feel like this is the kind of talk we need in regard to the area of purity. We need to be honest with ourselves in this area.

We're not after a purity in our own eyes, but a purity that God says is pure. We need to make sure that we are not only allowing God to *"create in us a clean and pure heart"* but that we are also in continual *pursuit* of purity.

We need to remind ourselves that we should not be basing our standards for purity on the current culture we live in. How many times do we find ourselves comparing ourselves to the world? "Well, it's not as bad as that." "I mean, look at what they are doing over there; I'm not doing anything nearly as bad as that." What we need to ask ourselves is: Am I pursuing purity as it relates to *the world*? Or am I pursuing purity as it relates to *the word*?

Psalm 119:9, instructs, *"How can a young person stay pure? By obeying your word"* (NLT). So apart from the word, there really is no purity.

I love what Romans 12:2 says in THE MSG translation:

> *Don't become so well-adjusted to your culture that you fit into it without even thinking. Instead, fix your attention on God. You'll be changed from the inside out. Readily recognize what he wants from you, and quickly respond to it. Unlike the culture around you, always dragging you down to its level of immaturity, God brings the best out of you, develops well-formed maturity in you.*

Too often we are becoming so well-adjusted to our culture that we are fitting into it without even thinking! Without even thinking we are allowing the enemy to steal our purity. Right before our eyes we are allowing the culture to drag us down to its own level of immaturity.

Our children are being stripped of their innocence (in more ways than one) at a younger and younger age. We've lost sight of what is pure.

So at some point we have to make a decision.

Do we sit back and continue to be a victim of the impurity of this culture allowing it to continue to affect our lives? Do we continue to base our standards for purity on the decaying culture in which we live? Or do we stand up and allow God to push the reset button in our hearts and lives in this area and begin to be *in pursuit* of purity.

The Little Areas

In a recent presidential election a particular candidate began to come under heavy scrutiny for an area of his life that was not very pure. This particular gentleman was coming under fire for some perverse, immoral areas in his past, specifically from those who were of the community of faith.

Now, understand, I'm not suggesting that as believers we don't stand up for what we believe in nor expect the highest moral standards out of our elected officials. I believe we should! But immediately when it was all going down and unfolding, I had the following thought: "When we as Christians publicly demean what we privately stream, nothing changes."

Our social media page screams "Pure! Pure! Raise the standard of Purity!" but our recently watched list on Netflix is not so convincing.

Philippians 4:8, says:

> *Finally, brothers and sisters, whatever is true, whatever is noble, whatever is right, whatever is pure, whatever is lovely, whatever is admirable—if anything is excellent or praiseworthy—think about such things.* (NIV)

You see it's the little things in life that really make the big difference. Song of Solomon 2:15 says, "*It's the little foxes that spoil the vine.*" We can't be deceived into thinking that the things we are continually digesting into our hearts and minds are not having an effect on us. Here a little impurity, there a little impurity—no biggie.

WRONG. It is having an effect.

It seems insignificant—one *border line* show, one *dicey* song, one snap with one *risky* friend—piece by piece they begin to chip away at our purity. And all it takes is one area, one open door, to allow the enemy to begin to steal away our purity. As the old saying goes, Samson didn't have to date an entire village to get a haircut.

It's difficult to be *in pursuit* of purity when I'm filling my heart and mind with thoughts that are not lining up with God's standard of purity.

Again, too often we are valuing a purity that is pure "*in our own eyes,*" and meanwhile our lifestyles reflect something that is so, so different from what God views as pure! He wants to do a work in our heart that changes us! God wants to do a work in us that we can't even comprehend, but it starts when we begin to value *purity* and allow God to *purify* our hearts and mind.

Remember, David said in Psalm 18:26, "*With the pure You will show Yourself pure.*" Now here's someone who knows about purity. David, a man who was considered a man after God's own heart, understood what purity was all about.

However, with that said, we see some pretty dark, nasty, impure parts of his life. David's fall with Bathsheba and all the events that surround this event in his life sound like the script of an X-Rated movie. However, pay attention to what David did in this darkest moment of his life. He responds to God with a very simple prayer of repentance that went like this, "*Create in me a pure heart, O God*" (Psalm 51:10, NIV).

So here's what we need to do.

We need to make a fresh commitment to be *in pursuit* of purity. What does this look like, you may ask? Being *in pursuit* of purity means:

I commit to not allow the brazenness of this culture to steal away my purity and innocence.

I commit to not set my standards for purity by the world, but rather by the Word.

I commit to allow God through the power of the Holy Spirit to restore unto me a pure heart and a pure mind.

Remember The Alamo

I think it's very fitting to end this chapter with a story that has become very familiar to me since moving to the great state of Texas a few years ago.

In December 1835, in the middle of Texas' war for independence from Mexico, a group of Texan volunteer soldiers occupied a former Franciscan mission known as the Alamo, located near the present-day city of San Antonio. Surrounded by a Mexican force numbering in the thousands, on February 23, 1836, the Alamo's 200 defenders began a valiant and courageous attempt to fight off the invading Mexican forces. Led by James Bowie and William Travis and including the likes of the famous Tennessee frontiersman Davy Crockett, the group courageously held on to the mission for 13 heroic days.

Finally, on the morning of March 6th, the Mexican invaders broke-through the outer wall and overpowered them, killing all of the Alamo's valiant defenders and only leaving behind a handful of survivors—mostly wives, children, and servants.

What seemed like such a tragic defeat, turned into an enduring symbol of hope. *"Remember the Alamo"* became the battle cry for commander Sam Houston and the remaining Texan forces heroically fighting for their independence. Just a few short months after the defeat of the Alamo, the Texans would win their revolution. As their army began their final attack on Santa Anna's Mexican army, their voices were lifted up in unison shouting, *"Remember the Alamo! Remember the Alamo!"*[1]

Yes, some days it feels like the "battle" for purity in our culture seems like a lost cause. It seems impossible, like we're losing on every front. But I believe with all my heart that in this day and hour God is awakening a generation who will be *in pursuit* of purity. A generation who will not see purity as a lost cause, but will rise and take a stand for and pursue purity.

When Daniel was dragged into a perverse, evil culture that was NOT his, scripture records, *"Daniel purposed in his heart that he would not defile himself with the portion of the king's delicacies"* (Daniel 1:8).

May the same be said of us.

We will not settle for the "delicacies" of a culture that does not live up to the standards of holiness and purity we see in God's word.

We will not bow down.

We will hold the fort for purity—and, no, it's not useless, for we are *in pursuit.*

141

IN PURSUIT OF POWER

*The Spirit-filled life is not
a special, deluxe edition of
Christianity. It is part and
parcel of the total plan of
God for His people.*

–A.W. Tozer

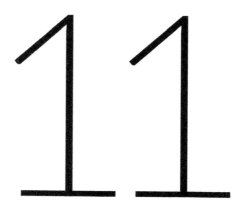

One of the greatest joys I've had as a father is to watch my children on their athletic teams. I've tried my best to at least be involved in some aspect of coaching (assistant or head coach) with each one of my children at least once, when they go out for sports.

Our youngest son Jaxon just started his athletic career this spring at the age of 4 by enrolling in *Blast-ball*. *Blast-ball* is a type of tee-ball, designed for younger age kids. It's like pre-school tee-ball, which, come to find out, is a lot like herding cats.

Anyway, with about seven 3- and 4-year-olds on a baseball field, whoever came up with the name was spot on, because it is a BLAST and absolutely hilarious to watch!

At one of our very first practices toward the beginning of the season, everything started off perfect. We (the coaches) called the little guys over onto the field and one of the coaches said, "Okay, Orioles, we are going to get started with practice so let's take a lap around the bases to get us all warmed up."

"Yay!!" they emphatically yelled as they threw their gloves in the air and made a dash to home plate.

One by one our little Orioles lined up behind coach at home plate and on his signal off they all went to first base. They arrived at first really quickly and one by one they touched first base (which in blast-ball the bases have a "honking" horn in them, which makes everything even more like a circus of sorts—it's INCREDIBLE). Next, they followed coach as he rounded first and made a sharp turn towards second—everyone, that is, except for Billy.

When everyone hung a left to go to second, Billy hung a right and ran to his car and never came back for the rest of practice.

NEVER.

Seriously, that was it.

Practice started at 6:00 PM (CST) and by 6:00:35 PM (CST) Billy was in the car. He was finished. Now he ran to first in a flash—incredible speed, but that was it, he had no interest in finishing!

I trust that this last chapter will bring a strong end to this call for radical believers to be *in pursuit*, and that we will finish this journey well.

The last thing that I want to leave you with that I'm convinced we must be *in pursuit* of is *power*.

Let's go briefly back to the start of this book, when I mentioned what the Lord had begun to speak to my heart in regards to *pursuit*. It was that phrase, from Matthew 24:37, "*As it was in the days of Noah, so it will be at the coming of the Son of Man*" (NIV).

Remember I shared that the Lord began to show me how that the increase of wickedness and ungodliness is only one sign of the last days. The other side of that coin, is the radical follower of Christ who will be absolutely abandoned in their pursuit of God and the things He loves—which this book has been about.

Well, in 2 Timothy 3:1-5, the Apostle Paul writes to his spiritual son Timothy, and he as well begins to reference what the last days will look like:

> But know this, that in the last days perilous times will come: For men will be lovers of themselves, lovers of money, boasters, proud, blasphemers, disobedient to parents, unthankful, unholy, unloving, unforgiving, slanderers, without self-control, brutal, despisers of good, traitors, headstrong, haughty, lovers of pleasure rather than lovers of God, having a form of godliness but denying its power.

Paul in this passage describes what the last days will look like and describes the wickedness that will begin to unfold. I believe we can all agree that we can testify of these things happening today right before our very own eyes! But what I want to point out to you is the last part of that passage. Verse 5 says that people will be, "*having a form of godliness but denying its power.*" Meaning they will look or appear to be "godly" people, but they will deny something very important that we must take note of—"power."

They would deny, reject, be in opposition to, one thing: Power.

The Greek word used for "power" here is, *dynamos* (doo'-nah-mos); which means: force, miraculous power—ability, abundance, meaning, might, power, strength, violence, mighty (wonderful) work. It is from this word that we get our English word, dynamite.

So catch this, Paul says that a key indicator of the last days is that people would "look the part" but they would deny or have nothing to do with "power," "*dynamos.*"

To fully grasp what Paul is saying, we need to look a little more at this word and where else it is used in scripture.

Luke 24:49 records the last earthly words of Jesus to his disciples:

> *Behold, I send the Promise of My Father upon you; but tarry in the city of Jerusalem until you are endued with power from on high.*

Note the word *power* here is the same word, *dynamos*.

Acts 1:8, reveals another one of Jesus' last instructions to His disciples: *"But you shall receive **power** when the Holy Spirit has come upon you."* Again, note the word *power* here is the same word, *dynamos*.

Why am I pointing this out to you? Is it to try and impress you with my Greek skills? Let me assure you, NO, we didn't speak a lot of Greek growing up in rural southwest Virginia. But rather, I point this out to help you see that, not only is it imperative that we are *in pursuit* of power, but more importantly, *that "power"* has a name, and it is the Holy Spirit.

We must be *in pursuit* of power, and that power is found in the person of the Holy Spirit.

Why would we settle for a form of godliness, without the power that was designed to go along with it? It's kind of like opening the most incredible gift or present, only to find out that it requires batteries and they didn't come with it. Another case of the infamous, "batteries not included" putting a damper on an incredible moment. No matter how awesome that toy or gift is, without the power required to cause it to function correctly, it's pretty much useless.

However, so many of us settle for the form without the power. Why is this?

I believe one of the main reasons is because we have so many misunderstandings about the Holy Spirit. I mean, let's be honest for a moment here. When someone mentions the name, "God," we're all fairly comfortable with it (sometimes too comfortable to be honest, but that's for another day). When someone says the name, "Jesus," it's pretty much the same. However, when someone says "Holy Spirit" or "Holy

Ghost" it's like someone flips on the cray-cray switch and everyone gets all nervous.

The truth is, we are talking about the same person! God the Father, God the Son, and God the Holy Spirit. The Holy Spirit is a person—He's God, and we don't have to be freaked out about Him or misunderstand Him or, more importantly, be afraid of Him! We need to be *in pursuit* of Him.

I love what Pastor Robert Morris says about the Holy Spirit, "The Bible never refers to the Holy Spirit as 'it'! The Bible always says He or Him!" So first and foremost if we are to be *in pursuit* of power, we need to understand that we are *in pursuit* of a Person and that person is God the Holy Spirit. We don't have to be afraid or confused or ashamed, but rather be *in pursuit* of Him.

THE BIG ONE

I don't know how the opening of Christmas gifts goes in your house, but in our house we kind of have a method or rhyme to the gifts that we give to our kids. Each year our kids will have one gift that is kind of their "big gift." It's more than likely the one thing they really wanted, or it's that extra special gift that Mom and Dad worked really hard to get.

Each year in our home that gift goes last, after all of the other presents have been opened. The anticipation builds, the excitement grows, and the last and final gift of the year is presented. Right before we hand it out, we reflect on all the gifts they've received so far.

We typically will say something like, "Man, you guys have had an awesome Christmas! Wow, we have so much to be thankful for!" Again, we know that the best is still yet to come. As a parent, this moment is almost as exciting for us as it is for the kids, because we know how hard we've worked to try to provide not just all of the gifts—but especially this last one.

The big one.

During Jesus' time here on earth and especially during His three years of ministry, He gave His disciples some pretty incredible stuff. The Gospels are full of His teaching, the wisdom and knowledge that He poured out was unprecedented. Unbelievable impartations into their lives. In other words, "It had been an incredible Christmas so far!"

But there was still one more gift yet to come. And this was a big one. The Father had a plan since the very beginning of time, and He had the perfect, last gift picked out for the disciples.

When Jesus mentioned to the disciples that He would be leaving soon, they were confused. This made no sense at all! Why? For what reason? What would they do without Him?

But He reassured them in John 16:7, "*Nevertheless I tell you the truth. It is to your advantage that I go away; for if I do not go away, the Helper will not come to you; but if I depart, I will send Him to you.*"

What seemed to the disciples as a hopeless situation, was really just a setup for God to reveal an incredible gift that He had prepared for them that was beyond anything they could imagine. They thought it was over; little did they know it was just beginning!

Then, not long after this very conversation, on the day of Pentecost, the promise of the Holy Spirit was poured out! Peter, stood up and said:

> *Repent, and let every one of you be baptized in the name of Jesus Christ for the remission of sins; and you shall receive the **gift of the Holy Spirit**.* (Acts 2:38)

God had one final gift for the disciples and it was a BIG ONE! The amazing thing is, that regardless of how some people feel or think about the Holy Spirit, that gift was NOT just for the disciples. Peter continues on, "*For the promise is to you and to your children, and to all who are afar off, as many as the Lord our God will call*" (Acts 2:38).

Here's what I've come to learn: **All means all.**

How much of a tragedy would it be if there, gathered around the Christmas tree, when presented with the last and final gift—"the big one"— my children would just completely ignore the gift? Turn their backs and walk away? Yet this is what so many believers do with the gift of the Holy Spirit! What a tragedy! They are missing out on a gift that Father God has handpicked just for them. In fact God has watched them—scoped them out—and He knows exactly what they need in order to live this God life here on earth, and so He gives them the precious gift of the Holy Spirit. But instead of receiving this gift, they settle for the form of godliness without the power. Others will open and receive this gift and the amazing joy that comes with it, however, fail to realize that this is not a one-time experience.

One time I had surprised my oldest son Chase by purchasing for him a brand new baseball bat. This was his first "really nice bat" and quite a step up from the Walmart clearance section bats he was used to swinging. He was getting a little more involved in baseball, a little more advanced, and I wanted him to have a better bat, so I saved up and got him one.

I didn't tell him I was purchasing it, I just came home with it one day. As he was getting ready to head out for practice, I showed him the bat (not telling him it was his), and I asked him what he thought about it. His eyes lit up as he gave it a few swings, and he couldn't believe how awesome it was. "Great!" I said, "it's yours and you can keep it forever— it's a gift."

How bad of a Father would I have been to give him this wonderful gift and only allow him to use it once?

The indescribable gift of the Holy Spirit is for you to experience and be *in pursuit* of on a daily basis! Your Dad loves you an awful lot—more than you could ever imagine—and He has the most incredible gift for you. You need this gift! We all need it. We need the help, guidance, and power of the Holy Spirit in our lives every single day.

I believe that the Lord is wanting to awaken a fresh desire in the hearts of his sons and daughters to be committed to live a Spirit-*filled* and a Spirit-*led* life. May the Holy Spirit not just be in our doctrine but in our daily life.

We daily receive the power that we need. We must seek to be led by the Holy Spirit in everything we do. I love what the scriptures record of the decision making of the early church leaders, "*For it seemed good to the Holy Spirit, and to us . . .*" (Acts 15:28). Notice who comes first in this equation.

Holy Spirit, then us.

So many times we reverse the roles to our own detriment.

THE GUIDE

One of my favorite places to travel in the world is to the nation of Brazil. Over the years I've come to love the Brazilian people and have been blessed with some wonderful friendships.

I'll never forget my first experience in Brazil with our mission team on a boat going up the Amazon River. We departed from Manaus, Brazil, and our captain navigated up through the largest river in the world. About eight hours after our departure, we were almost to the small village where we would be spending the next few days.

As the boat began to slow and the captain began to navigate the boat towards the village, we all of a sudden came to a stop. I thought we had arrived, but then I quickly realized that we were still in the middle of the river and our village was a few hundred yards away down a particular channel of the river. At first I thought, "Oh, man, we're gonna have to swim to shore," and to be honest, I wasn't quite ready for that!

The problem, was that our captain, even with all of his skills and knowledge needed a local to guide him through the twists and turns of the channel leading him back to our village. A few short minutes later out comes one of the locals in his small canoe and he began to guide our large boat slowly through the various twists and turns of the channel. You see in order to make it safely, we needed a guide—someone who had navigated these waters before. Someone who knew where the dangerous spots were—the potential pitfalls—and could carefully guide us through the obstacles to our destination.

In John 16, when Jesus was sharing with the disciples the importance of the person of the Holy Spirit, he said in verse 13, *"However, when He (the Holy Spirit), the Spirit of truth, has come, He will guide you into all truth."* The word guide, there is the Greek word *hodēgéō*, which means, "to show the way (literally or figuratively), to teach—guide, lead."

Why is it so imperative in this day and hour in which we live that we be *in pursuit* of the Holy Spirit? Because we are living in uncharted waters, and we need a guide! We need a *hodēgéō* to come alongside of us and guide us through life. We've never been this way before, but we have a helper, a guide, a teacher who is willing and ready to come alongside us and give us the power we need to make it along this journey.

Let's accept the help.

Let's take the guidance offered.

Let's receive the precious promise of the Holy Spirit and be *in pursuit* of power every single day!

CHAPTER 12

CONCLUSION (CHOP-CHOP)

We're not waiting on a move of God; we are a move of God.

–Steven Furtick

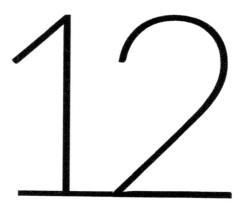

If you are waiting for a sign, THIS IS YOUR SIGN.

Today is the day to get moving, to kick it into high gear and be *in pursuit.*

God has tremendous plans for your life and has greatly invested in you. You are a part of God's plan here on earth.

Anyone with a pulse today is fully aware of how rapidly our society is moving away from God and the principles of His word. Many are walking away from the faith. This shouldn't come as a shock to us as believers. When Jesus was describing what the last days would be like, he said, *"At that time many will turn away from the faith"* (Matthew 24:10, NIV).

We are living in the last days—no doubt about it.

REMEMBER: As it was in the days of Noah, so it will be at the coming of the Son of Man.

As we close out this book, let's turn our attention to the bright side of this prophecy—and that my friend is YOU.

As you say, "YES," to God's purpose and plan for your life and choose to live a life *in pursuit*, you become a modern-day fulfillment of these prophetic words spoken over two thousand years ago. You become a modern day Noah—a radical follower of Christ willing to do whatever is asked of him. One who finds favor in the sight of the Lord and walks in close fellowship—*in pursuit!*

All you have to do is say, "Yes. Yes, God, I'm willing. I will be *in pursuit.*"

In Joshua 17, when Joshua is dividing the promised land to the tribes of Israel, the tribes of Ephraim and Manasseh come to Joshua with a request for more land. These two particular tribes were very large, and they felt like they needed more land. I love Joshua's reply:

> *And Joshua spoke to the house of Joseph—to Ephraim and Manasseh—saying, "You are a great people and have great power; you shall not have only one lot, but the mountain country shall be yours.* **Although it is wooded, you shall cut it down, and its farthest extent shall be yours;** *for you shall drive out the Canaanites,* **though they have iron chariots and are strong.*** (Joshua 17:17-18)

Joshua agrees to their request for more.

I believe God has MORE in store for us. I believe that we are going to experience God doing some incredible things in the last days, things beyond whatever we could ever think or imagine. I believe the word is true:

> *Most assuredly, I say to you, he who believes in Me, the works that I do he will do also; and greater works than these he will do.* (John 14:12)

However, these promises aren't going to just "happen." God doesn't operate that way. He chooses to use people—willing vessels. Joshua agreed to give them more, but he said, "You're going to have to pick up your axe and get to work."

Chop! Chop!

In other words: "I've got an incredible future for you, more than you could ever imagine, but I want to include you in it! Pick up your axe and let's get to work. Let's be *in pursuit* of the promises that God has laid before us!"

Let's bring the natural and let God take care of the SUPER.

No matter how big the obstacles may seem—we know what God has spoken—His word will not return void; it's time to get moving!

We will trust.

We will obey.

We are *in pursuit*.

Dear friend, all you have to do is say one simple word, "Yes."

I would like to end this book with a simple prayer from words of a song penned years ago by Ron Kenoly. If you would like to be *in pursuit*, I invite you to join me in this prayer:

Dear Lord,

If You can use anything Lord, You can use me.
If You can use anything Lord, You can use me.
Take my hands, Lord, and my feet.
Touch my heart, Lord, and speak through me.
If You can use anything Lord, You can use me.

Amen.

Now get going. This is your sign. Let's be, *in pursuit!*

END NOTES

CHAPTER 1

1. Larry Norman, "I Wish We'd All Been Ready," *Upon This Rock* (Capitol Records, 1969).

CHAPTER 3

1. Peter Chelsom "Dir.", Marc Klein "Wri.", *Serendipity* (Miramax, 2001). http://www.imdb.com/title/tt0240890/quotes (accessed March 18, 2017).

CHAPTER 4

1. Jon Santucci, *Tim Tebow Is Not a Baseball Player*, TC Palm: Part of the USA Today Network (Feb. 27, 2017). http://www.tcpalm.com/story/sports/mlb/spring-training/2017/02/27/jon-santucci-tim-tebow-not-baseball-player/98302462/ (accessed March 18, 2017).

2. Mark and Jill Herringshaw, *The Prayer of Sir Francis Drake*. http://www.beliefnet.com/columnists/prayerplainandsimple/2014/08/the-prayer-of-sir-francis-drake.html#xcK4UvYyl6EzYyoV.99 (accessed March 17, 2017).

CHAPTER 6

1. Wikipedia contributors. "Tactile paving." Wikipedia, The Free Encyclopedia, 17 Apr. 2017. (accessed March 20, 2017).

2. Iowa Hospital Association, "A Bridge Where the River Flows No More" (August 22, 2013) http://blog.iowahospital.org/2013/08/22/a-bridge-where-the-river-flows-no-more/ (accessed March 20, 2017).

INTRO TO PART 2

1. James C. Humes, *Speak Like Churchill, Stand Like Lincoln: 21 Powerful Secrets of History's Greatest Speakers* (New York: Three Rivers Press, 2002), 75.

CHAPTER 7

1. Cindy Wyatt, "Only One Life, 'Twill Soon Be Past – Poem by C.T. Studd." Poetry about Jesus and Salvation. (accessed March 24, 2017).

CHAPTER 9

1. David Maraniss, *When Pride Still Mattered: A Life Of Vince Lombardi* (New York: Touchstone, 1999).

2. Leonard Ravenhill, *Why Revival Tarries* (Bloomington: Bethany House, 1959, 1987), 25.

CHAPTER 10

1. History.com Staff, "*The Alamo*" (History.com, 2010) http://www.history.com/topics/alamo (accessed April 3, 2017).

IN PURSUIT

ACKNOWLEDGMENTS

When everything is said and done, I want those who know me the best, to love me the most. My family means the world to me. To my wife Dawn, I am grateful for the gift that God gave me in you. Thank you for saying "Yes" not only to me but more importantly to the call of God. Your love for God and our family is inspiring. To my kiddos, Chase, Maia, Cali, and Jaxon, you bring unspeakable joy to my life, and you always provide me with plenty of wonderful stories to write about! I can't tell you how much joy it brings me to actually see you read my books! May you increase in wisdom, knowledge, in the favor of God and man. This is our journey together.

To my parents, thank you for a lifetime of faithfulness, I am who I am today because of you.

Thank you for those of you who read my first book and encouraged me to keep writing.

Thank you to all those I've had the privilege of working with over the past ten years at the PCG International Offices. Your love for God is inspiring and I'm grateful for your impact on my life.

Thank you to Brian Ramos and Shy Rees for your insight and work on this project.

Thank you to the most incredible, awesome staff in the world at Messenger College and Impact PCG Student Ministries. Your dedication to the call of God inspires me to be *in pursuit!*

Finally, thank you to all of the leaders who have invested greatly in my life. You have pushed me to run faster, dig deeper, and never give up on being *in pursuit* of our high calling. I'm grateful for you.

ABOUT THE AUTHOR

Randy has a tremendous passion to serve his generation. He has served the body of Christ in a variety of leadership roles with global influence. He currently serves as the National Youth Director for the PCG, which leads over half a million Churches worldwide and he also serves as the president of Messenger College. He is a sought-after communicator and has devoted his life to recklessly pursuing God's call to reach this generation.

He holds a MA in Leadership and Management from Liberty University. Randy and his wife, Dawn, and their four children, Chase, Maia, Cali, and Jaxon reside in Fort Worth, Texas.

 @RANDALLKENTJR

IN
PURSUIT

RANDY LAWRENCE JR
FOREWORD BY WAYMAN MING

For more information on this book and other resources please visit:

WWW.RANDYLAWRENCEJR.COM

ALSO AVAILABLE:

RANDY LAWRENCE

THE BURN FACTOR

ALL FOR THE CALL

"We desperately need a generation of young people who will read *The Burn Factor* and discover the God who can do above and beyond what they dream possible. Parents, pastors, and youth leaders, please put a copy of this book in the hands of every young person in your care!"

Ron Luce, Founder and President of
Teen Mania International

"Getting to know Randy personally is a gift. His longing to see everyone step into their God-given call is not only relevant but crucial. We need a generation of Elijah's who will see the potential in others and a generation of Elisha's who will dare to believe God for greater things. Read this book prayerfully as it will fulfill an assignment in your life. The next chapter in God's story isn't just up to Him…it's up to you. Thank you, Randy, for being who you are and inviting us into an encounter."

Heath Adamson, National Youth Director Assemblies of God
and Author of
The Bush Always Burns

"*The Burn Factor* will awaken and stir the passion for Christ in your life. As you read Randy's personal stories and insights, you will find your heart yearning for God's "double portion" anointing for your life. This book will set you on a fresh journey of intimacy for Christ.

Richard Crisco, Senior Pastor Rochester First Assembly
and Author of
It's Time: Passing Revival to the Next Generation

Purchase your copy of *The Burn Factor* today at: